JOAN CHISSELL

SCHUMANN
Piano Music

BBC MUSIC GUIDES

ARIEL MUSIC
BBC PUBLICATIONS

Contents

Introduction

The piano was Schumann's own instrument. The first important girl in his life, Ernestine von Fricken, was a piano student. His great love and wife-to-be, Clara Wieck, was the finest young female pianist of her generation. It was scarcely surprising that he found it easier to express himself through the keyboard than any other medium, and was in fact content to publish nothing but piano music for the first ten years of his composing life. A few more miniatures followed as he grew older, among them three simple sonatas and other little pieces for his children. And he was never more at ease, in the increasingly ambitious projects of his later life, than when able to think through the piano again in songs, chamber-works and concerto-type pieces. But all his best-known, and indeed his finest, works for the solo piano belong to that remarkable first decade between his twentieth and thirtieth birthdays, 1830–40.

In spite of this, Schumann was far from being an 'Athena springing fully armed from the head of Zeus', to paraphrase his own famous phrase, in years to come, about the young Brahms. The number of juvenilia he rejected, and the elaborate processes of revision to which he subjected those early works considered worthy of preservation, are proof enough of the difficulties he experienced in youth in presenting his prodigious stream of ideas. For this, his own somewhat haphazard musical education was to blame. As a boy, his musical inclinations had been strongly encouraged by his father, who arranged piano lessons for him with Johann Gottfried Kuntzsch, the local Zwickau organist. But when August Schumann died in 1826, Robert's family insisted that his University training must be in the more secure profession of law. Both at Leipzig and Heidelberg Universities, where he studied in turn, many hours officially due to the lecture room were in fact spent at the piano – for in Leipzig Schumann was quick to start private lessons with the city's leading teacher, Friedrich Wieck. But it was not till 1830 that he persuaded his mother to let him abandon law for a six months' trial period with Wieck. Not unnaturally, at the age of twenty, Schumann found it more than difficult to start the kind of systematic technical training – both as regards keyboard technique and exercises in harmony and counterpoint – on which Wieck insisted. In spite of having achieved his heart's desire, the next few years found him persistently seeking short cuts. One of these, a mechanical contrivance for strengthening weaker fingers, eventually crippled his right hand and put an end to the virtuoso career that Wieck considered within his reach. As for his paper work, he obstinately refused to study with Weinlig, the erstwhile teacher of Wagner and also, more extensively, of Wieck's own daughter, Clara, who in 1830 was a prodigy of ten. He even came to grief in his lessons with a man of his own choosing, the younger and more progressive conductor of the opera, Heinrich Dorn, who 'wants to persuade me that music is nothing but fugues' – as Schumann soon complained. By 1832, in fact, impatience with everything academic had landed him with nothing but a treatise by Marpurg and Bach's *Well-Tempered Clavier* as his guides. All his early works, in consequence, were largely worked out at the piano through his own ten fingers.

There was never any doubt in Schumann's mind about the stature of Bach, Mozart, Beethoven and Schubert: countless diary entries prove that by 1831–2 they were his musical gods. On the other hand he could not, during his formative years, entirely overlook the exceptional popularity of virtuoso variations at that time in musical history, as written galore by such virtuoso-pianist composers as Hummel, Moscheles, Czerny, Marschner, Ries, Herz, Hünten, his own teacher Wieck, and countless others. Inevitably, as a young man, he felt impelled to try his hand at the same sort of thing. His sets on a theme of his own in G, on Schubert's *Sehnsuchtswalzer*, on the *allegretto* from Beethoven's Seventh Symphony and on Chopin's G minor Nocturne, Op. 15, no. 3, besides some four-hand variations on a theme of Prince Louis Ferdinand and a few for piano and orchestra on the *Rondeau à la clochette* theme from Paganini's B minor Concerto, remained in manuscript, but the best of them served as a kind of quarry for various later projects. Of the published works, only the C major *Toccata* (1829–32), the *Abegg Variations* (1830) and the *Concert Allegro* (1831) betray the influence of the note-spinning virtuoso style. Unorthodox and immature as his technique still was by the time he completed *Papillons* in 1832, Schumann already had a good idea where his own path lay.

Notes for their own sake as mere sound held little interest. Music for him could only be a language; he turned to the piano as others do to a diary, confiding to it all the innermost secrets of his emotional life. A letter to Clara in 1838 sheds valuable light on the workings of his musical mind:[1]

> I am affected by everything that goes on in the world and think it all over in my own way, politics, literature and people, and then I long

1 Extracts from letters and diaries of Robert and Clara Schumann are taken from Berthold Litzmann, *Clara Schumann: An artist's life based on materials found in diaries and letters* (London 1913) and from *Early Letters of Robert Schumann* (London 1888).

to express my feelings and find an outlet for them in music. That is why my compositions are sometimes difficult to understand, because they are connected with different interests; and sometimes striking, because everything extraordinary that happens impresses me, and impels me to express it in music. And that is why so few (modern) compositions satisfy me, because, apart from all their faults of construction, they deal in musical sentiment of the lowest order and in commonplace lyrical effusions.

In later years he looked back on these early years with some regret that 'the man and the musician in me were always trying to speak at once'. More than anything else, it was perhaps Mendelssohn's polished craftsmanship that opened his eyes to his own laboured technique when in the 1840s he turned to larger undertakings involving a mastery of sonata form. But as a young man it was the idea itself, symbolical of some very precise soul-state, that really mattered to Schumann. In his diary for 1831 he had even gone so far as to write:

whosoever has a beautiful thought, let him not worry it and caress it till it is vulgar and profaned, as many composers (like Dorn) do, calling this 'development'. If you want to develop, make something out of previous common-places – but don't commit that mortal sin.

He did in fact make a determined attempt on sonata-form in his middle twenties, but the best parts of the three sonatas he completed, not surprisingly, are the scherzos and slow movements: the faster flanking movements (involving sonata-form) betray all too clearly the difficulties he found in keeping afloat when launched into a sea of purely musical thought. The shorter spans of variation form, and more still, the character piece, either alone or strung into a suite (with or without a unifying theme), were his ideal outlets. Others, not forgetting Beethoven and Schubert, had written miniature mood-pictures before. But it was Schumann who brought the genre to fullest flower.

If the forms his keyboard music took were largely attributable to unorthodox training, the startling originality of its idiom was entirely the result of what Wieck once called his 'unbridled fancy', in other words his hyper-romantic imagination and desire to relate music to life. There was that brief encounter with the virtuoso school, there were passing nods at the waltz and polonaise rhythms of Schubert, but by his early twenties Schumann had already found a mode of expression uniquely his own. Even the Schubertian phase through which he passed was as much due to his early literary idol Jean Paul as to Schubert himself:

> Schubert is still 'my only Schubert', especially as he has everything in common with 'my only Jean Paul'. When I play Schubert I feel as if I were reading a romance of Jean Paul's set to music.

That is how he explained the situation to Wieck in 1829, as he sketched short pieces later to find a place in *Papillons*. What better musical way was there to evoke the atmosphere of the masked balls Jean Paul loved so well than by recourse to Schubertian dance rhythms?

Technically, Schumann's demands on his players are more modest than those of his notable contemporaries Liszt and Chopin – after the accident to his right hand his interest in virtuosity *per se* grew even less. He rarely used the extremes of the keyboard: he rarely exploited effects for their own sensuous beauty as sound. The floating, Italianate, often operatically inspired and operatically embellished style of melody favoured by Chopin and Liszt was entirely alien to his way of thought too. When writing 'vocal' melody, his inspiration was far more often the shorter-breathed *Lied*, shaped by the four-line stanza of verse. More often than not his melodies are woven into an active, arpeggio-based kind of figuration, the two hands never too far apart, often with off-beat echoes and limitations in other parts. His counterpoint he playfully claimed to have learned from Jean Paul, commenting to Clara:

> It is most extraordinary how I write almost everything in canon, and then only detect the imitation afterwards, and often find inversions, rhythms in contrary motion, etc.

However it came about, there is certainly a remarkable amount of inside activity within his closely woven texture, heightening the impression of hugged inner secrets. The frequent rhythmic surprises – syncopations, misplaced accents, conflicts of duple and triple time – that abound in the piano works can most easily be attributed to his interest in 'everything extraordinary'; similarly his startling changes of key, with enharmonic switches or sometimes totally unprepared plunges (particularly into keys a major third apart) completely disrupting the normal process of modulation through the orthodox circle of fifths. His piano works are also full of expression marks (not forgetting the most characteristic of all, *Innig* – intimate, warm, sincere) and constant changes of tempo again testifying to his mercurial temperament and urgent wish to communicate every passing shade of feeling.

Yet nothing could be less like programme music. Always Schumann loved to hide behind a mask. His secrets have to be prised out of mysterious hints and allusions in letters, literary and musical quotations, themes made out of letter names, the signatures of Florestan and/or Eusebius (his fictitious active and reflective selves) and goodness knows what else. Probably the only person who ever knew the whole truth was Clara. So much of what he wrote was directly addressed to her, during those dark days when Wieck forbade them to meet, forbade them even to correspond. Several of his themes were even ideas shared in happier days of her girlhood when, working alongside each other, they had indulged in an intimate process of musical cross-fertilisation. One particular five-note, step-wise descending melody stands out like a leit-motif of love and longing, but Schumann never named it publicly as such. In time, no doubt, researchers will have tracked down every clue. For the moment, however, it is because his music so constantly keeps us guessing that it remains so fresh.

The Early Years

Schumann's first prolific trying-out period lasted until about 1834. Much of what he wrote during these early years remained incomplete or unpublished, though quite a few extracts went through a drastic process of revision for future use: few composers have wrestled harder with their youthful ideas before presenting them to the world. The first group of published works comprises the *Abegg Variations, Papillons, Paganini Caprices*, six *Intermezzi, Impromptus on a Theme by Clara Wieck, Toccata* and *Allegro*.

ABEGG VARIATIONS, OP. I

> For the present I shall not go to Weimar. The fact is, I shall shortly be the father of a fine healthy child, at whose christening I should like to assist before leaving Leipzig. It will make its appearance at Messrs. Probst's, and heaven grant that you may understand it, with its first tones of youth and vivid life.

Schumann wrote these excited words to his mother from Leipzig in September 1831; the first-born-in-print appeared soon after. Most of the work on it had been done the previous year, when he was still ostensibly a law student at Heidelberg. As always he rejected as much as he selected from the original sketches, including drafts of an orchestral accompaniment of the kind the young Chopin had provided for his *Là ci darem* Variations, which Schumann so greatly admired.

Just as Chopin in his early variations was very much a child of his time, so Schumann here was influenced by the virtuoso style of performer-composers like Moscheles, Hummel, Herz and Czerny: their variations and concertos were compulsory study pieces for all of Wieck's piano pupils, and at this period in his life Schumann still thought himself destined to follow them. Yet even as a beginner he chose to follow fashion in his own very different way. His theme was no popular opera tune. Instead, he took it from the surname of a pretty dancing partner at a Mannheim ball, Meta Abegg, translated into musical notation:

Ex. 1

In his dedication he called her the Countess Pauline von Abegg, but that (according to Florence May)[1] was a mere smoke-screen, since the real

1 *The Girlhood of Clara Schumann* (London 1912), p. 58.

Meta was engaged to one of his friends. (Eric Sams even suspects Meta to be an anagram of *tema*.)[1] Apart from this early attempt to relate life and music, the musical reasoning in the variations also reveals that Schumann was striving for something more than decorative note-spinning. The opening of the first variation finds him prepared to detach the opening semitone for separate development, a process far more intensively pursued in the second variation, with its prophetic kind of syncopated patterning. Though the third variation resorts to fingerwork *per se*, imagination triumphs again in the delicately embellished fourth, where the switch into A flat is like the wave of a magician's wand. Virtuosity occasionally gets the upper hand in the finale, yet the 6/8 lilt keeps it airborne, and there are some bold harmonic excursions en route. Near the end there is an *ad libitum* reference to the theme's opening motif, with the held notes released one by one. This dying-away effect intrigued him a lot as a young man; he returned to it at the end of *Papillons*, and even made an exercise out of it in his preface to Op. 3.

PAPILLONS, OP. 2

In April 1832, six months after the appearance of Op. 1, the publishing house of Kistner brought out his Op. 2, *Papillons*. The title was apt, for nearly all twelve pieces in the suite underwent an elaborate process of metamorphosis, like larvae, before emerging in full butterfly grace and charm. There was a double edge to the symbolism in that Schumann claimed Jean Paul and the masked ball or *Larventanz* ('Larve' in German means mask as well as grub) in the last but one chapter of the novel *Flegeljahre* as his main source of inspiration. Nevertheless the dance rhythms running through the suite grew just as much from Schubert's waltzes and four-handed polonaises as from any literary ballroom.

Having hailed Jean Paul and Schubert as his idols (in the 1829 letter to Wieck quoted in the introduction), Schumann continued:

> I am also going to ask you to send me all Schubert's waltzes, and put them down to my account. I think there are ten or twelve books of them.

In next to no time he was composing waltzes of his own, sufficiently Schubertian in style to deceive even his closest friends, just as the year before he had written polonaises for piano duet (not published until

1 *Musical Times* (May 1966).

1933) closely modelled on those of his idol. Inevitably, then, it was to these Schubert-inspired dances he turned when Jean Paul eventually set him thinking of masked balls. After an arduous process of selection and revision, most numbers of the suite were then related to specific incidents in chapter 63 of *Flegeljahre*, where the brothers Walt and Vult (often considered the begetters of Florestan and Eusebius) exchange disguises at a ball to discover which of them their equally beloved Wina really loves. Schumann's marked copy of the novel survives as proof of this, though in a letter to Henriette Voigt he was at pains to emphasise that he adapted the text to the music and not vice versa, except for the finale which was a deliberate evocation of the masquerade in general.

Some of the connections are difficult to discern. Others are immediately recognisable, such as the 'aurora-borealis sky full of crossing, zig-zag figures' of no. 2, and the bare octave tune of no. 3 depicting Jean Paul's 'What most of all attracted him and his astonishment was a giant boot that was sliding around, dressed in itself'. In a letter to a friend Schumann even described it as the 'seven-league boot in F sharp minor'. Similarly the uprising octave motif in no. 1, requoted in the finale (as well as in 'Florestan' from *Carnaval* and in the *Davidsbündlertänze*) is easily identifiable with Jean Paul's words: 'He felt like a hero, thirsting for fame, who goes forth to his first battle':

Ex. 2

The finale itself sets out with the old *Grossvatertanz* as its main theme, the tune (traditionally played at the end of a ball) which Schumann chose again to caricature the Philistines, routed by the 'David club', at the end of *Carnaval*:

Ex. 3

Nothing in *Papillons* is more imaginative than the ending, as the clock chimes six and the sounds of revelry fade into the distance; Schumann even pares away the notes of his sustained dominant-seventh chord one by one (the same effect embryonically exploited in the finale of the *Abegg*

Variations) before the throw-away cadence. His first copy of *Papillons* is said to have been prefaced, as an explanatory motto, by the closing words of *Flegeljahre*: 'Hark, from the distance Walt listened in rapture to the fleeing notes; for he did not realise that his brother was fleeing with them.'

Critics were of course baffled by the aphoristic nature of the pieces, and their eccentrically swift-changing keys, tempi and rhythms. Schumann anticipated this in his diary for 1831 when remarking on

> quick changes and motley colours so that the listener still has the previous page in his head while the player has already finished. This 'self-obliteration' of the *Papillons* may perhaps be open to criticism but is certainly not inartistic.

But the most perceptive critics, notably Grillparzer, also recognised that here was someone who could create a 'new and ideal world for himself in which he revels almost recklessly'. And a letter Schumann wrote to his mother reveals that he himself was fully aware of a 'certain independence' striving to assert itself as he wrote his music. Retrospectively, we are in a better position to explain the source of that independence: in *Papillons* Schumann took his first steps away from pure notes into the world of ideas. The dedicatees were his three sisters-in-law, Therèse, Rosalie and Emilie.

In view of Clara's subsequent role in Schumann's life, it is interesting that she almost immediately replied to *Papillons* with an Op. 2 of her own in dance style entitled *Caprices en forme de Valse*. It, too, has a dying-away effect at the end of no. 2. She makes much play with an uprising motif perhaps suggested by Schumann's 'hero' (Ex. 2). Most important of all, her no. 7 includes a *doloroso* reference in F minor to a falling figure soon to become her 'motto-theme' in Schumann's music:

Ex. 4

STUDIES AFTER CAPRICCI BY PAGANINI, OP. 3
CONCERT STUDIES ON CAPRICES BY PAGANINI, OP. 10

On Easter Sunday 1830 Schumann went with two friends to Frankfurt to hear Paganini. The experience bowled him over even more than an outstanding piano recital by Moscheles eleven years before, and early in 1832, while still much preoccupied with problems of piano technique, he arranged six of Paganini's famous 24 *Capricci per il violino solo* as keyboard studies. To his recently departed harmony and counterpoint teacher, Dorn, Schumann wrote on 25 April 1832:

> I missed your help very much in arranging Paganini's Caprices for the piano, as the basses where often doubtful; but I managed to get on by keeping everything very simple.

A fortnight later he had still more to tell Wieck:

> They were a delicious but rather herculean work. Please take a pencil, sit down next to Clara, and mark whatever strikes you. . . . The preface will be finished in about three days. I have got such a quantity of materials for it, that I cannot be slow and careful enough about making my choice.

The preface is almost a piano tutor in itself, interesting for the light it sheds on Schumann's own approach to technique. 'A very exact and carefully considered' fingering comes first in his scheme of priorities. After it he stresses buoyancy and mellowness of tone, finish and exactness of the individual parts, flow and lightness of the whole. His comments on the specific technical problems inherent in each piece are accompanied by preparatory exercises of his own – designed, he modestly adds, only as a stimulus to the player to invent new ones for himself. A letter sent to the critic, Rellstab, with the review copy ('a sample for the critics of what I can do in theory') makes it clear that Schumann knew Paganini's harmonies were sometimes ambiguous and that occasionally the Caprices were imperfect in form and symmetry. Yet out of respect for this great artist he kept as near as possible to the original in his arrangements, making only very small modifications (such as omitting the middle of no. 3) and alterations of figuration in accordance with the demands of the keyboard. Later he realised this was a mistake, that arrangements of this kind need not be merely pedagogic. Though he had assured Rellstab that he would 'rather write six of my own than again arrange three of anybody else's', the following year he found it impossible to resist the challenge anew, in the light of the truth that had dawned.

The six pieces of his Op. 10 are significantly called not just studies, but *concert* studies, and Schumann introduced them in this way:

When I formerly edited a book of studies after Paganini, I copied the original, perhaps to its injury, almost note for note, and merely enlarged a little harmonically. But in this case I have broken loose from a too closely imitative translation, and striven to give the impression of an original pianoforte composition, which, without separating itself from the original poetic idea, had forgotten its violin origin. It must be understood that in order to accomplish this, I was obliged to alter and do away with much, especially in regard to harmony and form, but it was done with all the consideration due to such an honoured spirit as Paganini's.

For no. 2, for instance, he found a different accompaniment, fearing the original tremolo would 'fatigue players and hearers too'. No. 3 he suspected might not sound quite showy enough, in relation to the difficulty of playing it. In the working out of no. 4 he confessed that the funeral march from Beethoven's *Eroica* was constantly in his mind; this whole number is full of romanticism. In no. 5 he admits to having

intentionally omitted the marks of expression, leaving students to find out its heights and depths for themselves. This will afford a good opportunity for testing the scholar's power of comprehension.

For no. 6 he offers practical advice for the left hand's crossed high notes – 'the chords sound fullest when the crossing finger of the left hand sharply meets the fifth of the right hand' – but is mainly concerned to give warning that the piece may not be immediately recognised as a Paganini Caprice – for harmonic and other reasons which he specifies in self-justification.

When called upon to review Liszt's efforts in the same field a few years later, Schumann at once put his finger on the difference between his own Op. 10 and Liszt's *Paganini Studies*. Whereas he had stressed poetry, Liszt (without entirely ignoring the poetry) had deliberately met Paganini on his own ground in pushing his instrument's virtuoso potential to its limit:

Liszt correctly entitles the pieces 'bravura studies', such as may be performed in public for the purpose of display. The collection is probably the most difficult ever written for the pianoforte, as its original is the most difficult work that exists for the violin. To be sure, very few will be able to master them, perhaps only four or five in the world.

Even in Liszt's subsequent, slightly simplifed version (1851) of his pieces there are technical challenges undreamed of by Schumann; players have always preferred them to Schumann's set for their richer exploitation of keyboard texture and colour. But Schumann's comparatively modest Op. 10 was prophetic of his own future. Expressiveness, rather than flamboyant gesture, was to remain an ideal for life – and not just because of his own lamed hand.

INTERMEZZI, OP. 4

Writing to his old law-student friend, Theodor Töpken, on Good Friday 1833, Schumann remarked how glad he was Töpken had discovered *Papillons*, 'since many of them originated in the neighbourhood of beautiful Heidelberg and in your company'. But in the next sentence he drew Töpken's attention to the imminent publication of the *Intermezzi*, written in 1832, which he described as 'extended *Papillons*'. That he was proud of the extra length is confirmed by a subsequent diary entry, when after misguidedly dismissing his earliest efforts as 'too small and rhapsodic to make a fuss about', he then singled out the *Intermezzi* (together with the *Toccata*) as showing 'more serious effort'. This he attributed to his brief studies with Dorn (who nevertheless had thrown up the struggle with so wayward a pupil in April 1832) and to the beneficial influence of Bach.

Except for the fourth of the set, each of the *Intermezzi* has a contrasting middle section called *alternativo* (sometimes, but not always, thematically linked), after which the opening material is recapitulated, often with ingenious incidental transformations. For the shorter fourth piece in C, Schumann resurrected one of his adolescent excursions into song, a setting of his own poem 'Hirtenknabe', which with several others he had sent for criticism to Wiedebein in 1828. (Two more were to be reincarnated in the F sharp minor and G minor Piano Sonatas.) For the connecting links between the verse melody in no. 4, Schumann raided two other unpublished juvenilia, a Piano Quartet and a rejected *Papillon*. Another discarded *Papillon* provided him with the charming 3/4 D major *alternativo* for the sixth of the set, whose agitated B minor opening and closing sections include a startling swerve into unexpected tonality near the end so as to quote the A, B flat, E, G, G motif in its original notation.

The *Abegg* quotation is not the only hint of latent romantic undercurrents in these pieces, for which Schumann first chose the title *Pièces phantastiques*. In no. 2 in E minor, the Goethe words 'Meine Ruh' ist hin' (Gretchen's song in *Faust*) are written over the main motif of the *alternativo* (recalled at the very end) as a clue to the unrest of the opening and closing sections (which suggest that Schumann knew and loved the *allegretto* of Beethoven's Op. 10, no. 2). As for the fifth Intermezzo, Boetticher in his *Robert Schumann in seinen Schriften und Briefen* has tracked down a revealing diary entry: 'The opera without text – but my whole heart is in thee, dear fifth Intermezzo, that was born with such unutterable love.'

In letter as well as spirit the *Intermezzi* are forward-looking: they abound in cross-rhythms and syncopation (especially nos. 2 and 5), in concealed inner threads, and last but not least in harmonic adventure. But very often Schumann seems to be experimenting for its own sake. Whether he learnt his counterpoint from Jean Paul (as he claimed), or Dorn, or Bach, he is too anxious to show off his accomplishment in this respect in no. 1, where contrapuntal imitation becomes an end in itself. Many of his short-cut modulations sound equally contrived, notably in nos. 2 and 4, but also once or twice in the *alternativo* of no. 5, and certainly in that wrench to bring back the *Abegg* theme in its original key near the end of the B minor section of no. 6. For finished craftsmanship, as well as romance, nos. 2 and 5 are probably the most worthy of rescue. The key sequence of the six pieces, plus three *attacca* markings, suggest that Schumann himself expected them to be played as a set.

IMPROMPTUS ON A THEME BY CLARA WIECK, OP. 5

In the summer of 1833 Schumann started work on a set of variations (or impromptus, as he preferred to call them) on a *Romance* by Clara – on which she also wrote variations to dedicate to him as her Op. 3. He dedicated his own work to Wieck, getting it published privately at his brother's printing-house in a very great hurry so that it should arrive as Wieck's forty-eighth birthday present. Clara at this time was only a child of thirteen: she adored her 'moon-struck maker of charades' like an elder brother; he was as fond of this *Wunderkind* as of a little sister. That was all. But the fact that Schumann returned to these youthful *Impromptus* in 1850 to revise them extensively suggests that retrospectively he might have recognised this first mating of their musical ideas as a major landmark in a lifetime of cross-fertilisation.

The strong bass to Clara's theme in Schumann's Op. 5 is not hers but his. Its opening motto of falling fifths could well have been suggested by those of her tune. Yet he himself first refers to it in a diary entry as early as 29 May 1832:

> This evening I tore through six Bach fugues, arranged as duets, at sight, with Clara . . . and when I came home, about 9 o'clock, I sat myself down at the piano and ideas poured from me till veritable flowers and gods seemed to stream from my fingers. The idea was C F G C:

Ex. 5

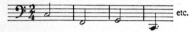

In spite of Schumann's several references to the influence of Bach at this period of his life, the importance of the bass throughout his Op. 5 indicates that he also knew and admired Beethoven's E flat (*Prometheus*) variations. Naturally, his 1850 revisions include several instances of superior craftsmanship: by this time he had learnt where simplification could clarify and strengthen, notably in nos. 2, 3 (a complete reincarnation) and 7. He knew where to reinforce, as in the use of chords rather than bare octaves to accentuate the syncopation in no. 6 (where incidentally he also omitted eight bars recalling Clara's tune in the tenor). He removed his original penultimate variation in F minor – A flat major altogether, as if in awareness that its romanticism lacked the classical succinctness of the rest. He also substituted a rather more formal and conclusive ending to the fugal finale, as if suspecting that after diligent strettos, inversions, and so on, his original *Papillons*-like fading away into nothingness was altogether too fey.

In sum, these *Impromptus* reveal him as a composer still in search of a style. Yet his respect for Bach and Beethoven gave him a strong lead over Clara, whose own Op. 3 variations remain innocently decorative, in the virtuoso style. But one passage in Clara's work cannot pass unremarked. Just before the brilliant ending, there is a brief *lento e piacere* interlude introducing the falling figure already noted in another form in her Op. 2 (see p. 13).

TOCCATA IN C, OP. 7
ALLEGRO IN B MINOR, OP. 8

The opus numbers of these two bravura-type pieces suggest that Schumann had given up his search for new paths and returned to the virtuoso camp; in point of fact both were conceived before he had really left it. The piece that emerged in 1834 as the *Toccata in C*, Op. 7, with a dedication to Schumann's close friend, Ludwig Schunke, was first envisaged as a D major *Étude fantastique en doubles-sons* (intended for Clara) as far back as 1829, when Schumann was still intoxicated with Moscheles in Heidelberg. Its revisions were in a good cause, for as we now know it the *Toccata* assembles a great variety of technical teasers – double notes, octaves, repeated notes requiring rapid finger changes, wide skips, contrasts of *legato* and *staccato* and of *ff* and *pp* – within a succinctly disciplined framework of classical sonata form (his first essay in this medium).

The *Allegro* began as the first movement of a sonata in B minor at which Schumann worked throughout the winter of 1831–2 in the hope of dedicating it to Moscheles; in the event he published only this one movement, in 1833, with a dedication to Ernestine von Fricken. (An earlier A flat sonata experiment was totally suppressed.) Sketches show that the *Allegro* gave him a great deal of trouble: he himself subsequently dismissed it as having 'little to commend it beyond good intentions'. In trying to organise such rhapsodic material into a sonata-form argument Schumann was in fact attempting the impossible. But that a search for unity was among his good intentions is very clear: it is interesting to discover how much in the discursive argument can be traced back to the introduction. The transformation of its disturbed B minor opening gestures into a benignly glowing B major at the end is very beautiful. The subject-matter is borne along on a stream of improvisational fancy rather than truly developed, yet Schumann's unpredictable enharmonic modulation in the central section certainly results in startling variety of colour.

On the Crest of the Wave

Much of Schumann's time in 1834 was taken up with the launching of the *Neue Zeitschrift für Musik*, a progressive journal aimed against pedagogues and virtuoso pedlars of the day, in an attempt to awaken interest in the great and glorious past and to 'hasten the dawn of a new poetic age'. As editor he assembled all his like-minded friends, under fictitious names, into an imaginary league of Davidites to attack the Philistines. A novel he had abandoned gave him his own two pseudonyms, Florestan and Eusebius, standing for the active and contemplative sides of his dual nature. When he returned to manuscript paper, it was no longer *in statu pupillari*, but with a clearly formed artistic aesthetic: the *Davidsbund* flag flew over his compositions as over all his other activities. 1834–8 saw the birth of his eight most substantial works for the piano, *Carnaval, Études symphoniques*, the three Sonatas, *Fantasia in C, Davidsbündlertänze* and *Kreisleriana*. In some he actually attributed the authorship to Florestan and Eusebius. All are inextricably mixed with his personal life.

CARNAVAL, OP. 9

As for composing, it naturally proceeds more leisurely . . . just now I have to devote my whole energy to the paper [Schumann wrote to his mother on 2 July 1834, ending with a confidence]: added to this, two gorgeous women have entered our circle. I told you before of Emilia, the 16-year-old daughter of the American consul. . . . The other is Ernestine, daughter of a rich Bohemian, Baron von Fricken – her mother was a Gräfin Zettwitz – a wonderfully pure, childlike character, delicate and thoughtful. She is really devoted to me, and cares for everything artistic. She is remarkably musical – everything, in a word, that I might wish my wife to be. A whisper in my dearest mother's ear – if the future asked me whom I would choose I would answer with decision 'This one'.

Ernestine had come to Wieck's house in Leipzig as pupil and boarder. In time Schumann discovered she was illegitimate, and not quite as artistically or intellectually distinguished as love had first persuaded him to believe. Eventually he jilted her – but fortunately not before she had provided him with the imaginative spur he then needed for a major composition.

Schumann's close friend and confidante at the time was Henriette Voigt, who often helped him to meet Ernestine without Wieck's knowledge. All this romantic excitement at first only revived Schumann's interest in some variations he had started in 1833 on Schubert's *Sehnsuchtswalzer*, to which he now liked to refer as 'musical love-stories' and planned to publish as *Scenen* with a dedication to Henriette. Suddenly everything took a new turning in the light of a startling discovery: Ernestine was born in Asch, and SCHA were the very four letters in his own name which could be translated into musical notation (in German: E flat, C, B natural, A). The coincidence seemed to seal his destiny, and though not entirely forgetting Schubert in 3/4 time, he started writing entirely new variations. By 1835 they were complete, under the title *Fasching: Schwänke auf vier Noten* (Carnival: Jests on four notes). The work was subsequently published as *Carnaval: Scènes mignonnes sur quatre notes*, with a dedication not to Ernestine or Henriette, but to the violinist-composer Karol Lipiński.

Whereas Abegg permitted only one musical spelling, Asch invited three, which Schumann sets out in the course of the work (after 'Réplique') in mysterious breves entitled *Sphinxes*, presumably intended to be seen but not heard:

Ex. 6

(i) Es - C - H - A (ii) As - C - H (iii) A - Es - C - H

Except for *Préambule*, whose opening twenty-four bars were taken from the rejected Schubert *Scenen*, all the variations make use of the motto in some form or other, most often with an overt reference to the chosen spelling at the outset, but sometimes holding it back until later (as when Ex. 6 (i) arrives almost incidentally in the second half of *Chopin*) or with vital notes surreptitiously woven into new tunes (as in *Eusebius*) or textures (as in *Paganini*). In *Reconnaissance* the motto is even the excuse for one of those startling, short-cut enharmonic key-switches Schumann loved so much in youth, here from A flat major into B major for the middle section. The brevity of all three motifs presented Schumann with a new challenge. The purely decorative kind of variation was no longer possible: there had to be some kind of organic growth. And the burgeoning of the A flat, C, B natural motif as in Ex. 6 (ii) of *Chiarina*, with ever widening intervals and an important countersubject, is just one instance of how he was gradually acquiring the knack of allowing ideas to develop. His invention even overflowed into five variations for which there was no place in *Carnaval*; they emerged many years later in the miscellaneous collections of Op. 99 and Op. 124.

Though the intrinsic musical unity is much closer than in *Papillons*, again in this suite Schumann resorted to an extra-musical *Maskentanz* as a means of making the whole add up to more than the sum of its parts. Some of the dancers wear *commedia dell' arte* disguise; others are recognisable enough to make it difficult to believe that Schumann was speaking the truth to Moscheles, some two years later, when saying that he added the titles after writing the music. *Chopin, Paganini,* and Schumann himself in the roles of *Florestan* and *Eusebius,* are particularly lifelike. In *Florestan* he quotes an uprising octave phrase from the first number of *Papillons*, associated with Jean Paul's 'he felt like a hero, thirsting for fame, who goes forth to his first battle' (see Ex. 2). Clara's portrait (*Chiarina*) is of equal interest for its hidden, descending counter-melody (A flat, G, F, E flat, D). Twice already a similar falling phrase had appeared in her own works (see pp. 13 and 18). Here Schumann seems to be making his first, tentative use of it as her 'motto'. Ernestine (*Estrella*) is of course among the dancers, but surprisingly not Henriette – or at any rate not under either of her *Davidsbund* names of Eleonore and Aspasia. The *Davidsbündler* arrive in force at the end to march (provocatively in 3/4 time) against the Philistines, who again, as in *Papillons*, are caricatured by the seventeenth-century *Grossvatertanz*.

'A higher kind of *Papillons*' was Schumann's own summarisation of *Carnaval*, and it cannot be bettered. Apart from the similar connecting thread, there is the same spontaneous charm of material, the same sense of proportion and directness in its presentation, but all at a more fully developed level. Significantly, however, Schumann never put quite so many of his cards face upwards on the table again.

ÉTUDES SYMPHONIQUES, OP. 13

The *Études symphoniques* also owes its existence to the Fricken episode in Schumann's life, though this time the starting-off point was not Ernestine but her guardian (and natural father), the Baron von Fricken. He was a keen music-lover, amateur flautist, and would-be composer too, for in the summer of 1834 he sent Schumann a set of variations he had just completed for the flute, inviting the opinion of his prospective son-in-law. Schumann not only responded in September 1834 with a detailed and remarkably astute criticism of the Baron's efforts, but also began to write variations of his own on the Baron's theme, a set which after many changes of mind (even as regards title and authorship: *Zwölf Davidsbündler Etuden* and *Etuden im Orchester Charakter, von Florestan und Eusebius* were both considered) eventually emerged in print in 1837, under his own name, as *Études symphoniques*. Even then Schumann was not completely satisfied, for in 1852 he brought out a second edition from which he omitted the third and ninth numbers, besides revising the finale and altering the collective title to *Études en forme de variations*. The edition most commonly used now is a posthumous one of 1862, which reinstates the third and ninth numbers but retains the tautened 1852 finale.

As we know it today, this work is one of Schumann's most majestic bravura works. But Schumann's letter to the Baron suggests that he set out with a completely different aim. His main criticism of that gentleman's variations was that they were too alike in character:

> No doubt the subject ought always to be kept well in view, but it ought to be shown through different coloured glasses, just as there are windows of various colours which make the country look rosy like the setting sun, or as golden as a summer morning. . . . [The revealing point followed.] I am now really arguing against myself, as I have actually been writing variations on your theme, and am going to call them 'pathetic'. Still if there is anything pathetic about them, I have endeavoured to portray it in different colours.

In a manuscript (known as the Berlin sketch) showing Schumann's first attempts to pull the work into shape, the theme is in fact labelled 'Tema quasi marcia funebre'. Of the ten variations that followed (in various stages of completion), only two – plus a few scraps – found a place in the 1837 publication. But five others, in more fully developed form, are familiar as a result of Brahms's decision to salvage them by including them as an independent group in the supplementary volume of the Breitkopf Complete Edition. That Schumann rejected ideas as beautiful as these can only be explained by the fact that they are all predominantly nostalgic and reflective, too much alike to bring the variety he had already accused the Baron of failing to achieve. In a second letter to the Baron in November 1834, he did in fact confess that he was experiencing paralysing difficulties in trying to escape from the minor mode, in getting the necessary dramatic contrast, and in finding a way of working up the funeral march into a triumphal victory march by way of conclusion. Gradually, it seems, the 'pathetic' conception of the work gave way to something much less broodily improvisational, something more symphonic (in terms of organic growth) and at the same time more alive to the piano's virtuoso potential. In this latter respect, it is tempting to wonder if Chopin played some of his own *Études* to Schumann when visiting him in Leipzig in September 1836. Certainly an entry in Schumann's diary reads: 'the whole day of September 18 at the piano, composing *études* with great gusto and excitement'. *Études*, it should be noted, not variations; gusto and excitement, not pathos. It was certainly Schumann's friendship with the twenty-year-old Sterndale Bennett a bit later that autumn that brought an unexpected solution to the problem of the triumphal finale. As a tribute to Bennett, the work's eventual dedicatee, Schumann allowed himself the luxury of a brand-new motivating idea at this point – the phrase 'Du stolzes England, freue dich' ('Proud England, rejoice') from Marschner's *Ivanhoe* opera, *Der Templer und die Jüdin*.

Schumann's initial presentation of his theme is concentrated and direct. This, he felt, was a matter of vital importance, as we know from his first letter to the Baron:

> I object also to the material of the [i.e. your] theme, as savouring too much of a variation. . . . I should like it simpler – in fact in its original form. My own idea as to what it should be is expressed in the enclosed, and perhaps Fräulein Ernestine will play it to you. I have always been very strict as regards themes, because the entire construction depends upon them.

He certainly had no enthusiasm for the Baron's use of an introduction before the first statement of the theme:

> Besides beginning in an unrelated key, it contains too little preparation, indeed, it even lessens the impression which the grave simple theme would make if it began by itself.

Though he liked the Baron's original use of a free, connecting ritornello en route, he did not adopt it himself: each of his own variations is separate and self-contained while yet a vital link in the chain, placed with a keen ear for contrast alike of key, pace and texture. Nos. 3 and 5 both gravitate towards the relative major of E, as if in preparation for the brilliant seventh variation which makes E major its home. The ruminative eleventh *étude* moves into G sharp minor, and the triumphal finale is in the tonic major enharmonically respelt as D flat. Pianistic as they are, the textures evoke orchestral timbre more keenly than much of Schumann's keyboard music (his dalliance with the title *Etuden im Orchester Charakter* suggests that he was not unaware of this). And while offering splendid scope for virtuosity, never once does Schumann resort to purely decorative note-spinning around his theme: new facets are revealed in each variation. Sometimes the theme's outline is clearly preserved, as when supporting (in the bass or tenor) the grandiloquent new melodic gestures of the second *étude*, or when syncopated amidst the *con bravura* figuration of the sixth (a patterning taken over from his unpublished variations on the *allegretto* from Beethoven's Seventh Symphony). Even the canonic fourth *étude* leaves no possible doubt about its parentage. Sometimes, though, Schumann allows the merest snippet from the theme to generate new ideas, and notably the initial falling fourth which grows into the fugato-like subject of the first *étude* (which the Berlin sketch reveals as originally designated for the finale), and later into the richly romantic song of the eleventh. Several of the numbers are free enough to make it clear why Schumann was chary of calling the work a set of variations. Once or twice on these occasions a falling arpeggio suddenly rings out of the blue as a salutary reminder that Schumann has never really forgotten the theme – and especially in the episodes of the Marschner-inspired finale. Obsessive dotted rhythms in these episodes would have benefited from still more pruning in the second edition. But the climactic *fff* chord of B flat major twenty bars before the end, its D natural cutting through the D flat major tonality like a great flare of light, is a masterstroke which never palls.

To insert the five rejected variations into a complete performance of the *Études symphoniques*, as many players nowadays do, is to ignore Schumann's three-year struggle to find his ideal form for the work. In comparison with the close reasoning of what he chose to publish in 1837, these early musings are very much the kind of music he might have improvised around the Baron's theme while dreaming about 'Fräulein Ernestine'. Clara, it seems, was much against their publication. Her diary for May 1873 records:

> I copied out some symphonic studies which were left among Robert's papers, for Simrock, as he wished to print them as a supplement to the others. I was very much against it from the first, but I was so urged to do it that at last I agreed.

No one today is likely to question the wisdom of printing them; they are far too beautiful to waste. But they are better played as an independent group.

SONATA IN F SHARP MINOR, OP. 11

The sufferer throughout the Ernestine von Fricken episode was Clara. A long concert tour during the winter of 1834–5 helped to divert her thoughts from her erstwhile hero; back in Leipzig in April 1835 she found the situation slightly eased by Ernestine's departure (though still officially Schumann's fiancée) to her home town of Asch. So throughout the whole of the summer of 1835 Robert and Clara were almost daily in each other's company, resuming the relationship they had enjoyed during the very happy summer of 1833. Both were aware of a deepening sympathy, but for the moment were still content to let it find outlet in music. And by September 1835 Clara was the proud possessor of a sonata inscribed 'To Clara, from Florestan and Eusebius'.

Like so much of Schumann's early music, the first two movements had completely different origins. The first movement grew from a Fandango which Hoffmeister, the publisher, was expecting in January 1833. But as Schumann explained to Hoffmeister, 'Together with these lines I am sending you an *Allegro di bravura*. Perhaps you would like it instead of the Fandango, as I lost a sheet of that some time ago, and up to now have not found the thread again.' When the missing sheet was (presumably) found, not only Schumann 'picked up the thread'. Clara's *Quatre Pièces caractéristiques*, Op. 5, includes as its no. 4 a piece called 'Le Ballet des revenants' based on the same two opening motifs of Schumann's Sonata, the punctuating fifths:

Ex. 7
(i) CLARA

(ii) ROBERT

and the fandango-type rhythm:

Ex. 8

(i) CLARA

(ii) ROBERT

Her piece is naturally much more simply expressed, alike in form and texture, and uses not F Sharp minor but B minor. This possibly explains the reference to key in her proudly grateful letter of thanks to Schumann – which nevertheless contained a plea for some simplification of his work, or as she put it, 'some further modification at the end of its enchanting tones: "B minor instead of F sharp minor".'

Trying to convert dance measures into a sonata-form argument presented Schumann with problems not wholly overcome. The fandango rhythm of the first subject is grossly overworked. The smooth-flowing A major second subject arrives late and even then is too brief to bring adequate contrast. This second subject finds no place at all in the richly ornate, sequential development, where the only relief from first-subject matter is provided by a rather contrived recall of the opening motif of the introduction. The *poco adagio* introduction itself was not part of the fandango: the beautiful melody which eventually grows from its initial brooding was in fact borrowed from the Aria slow movement in an attempt to impose some kind of kinship on these two quite separately conceived movements.

The Aria is a fairly close A major transcription of one of the songs (salvaged by Brahms in the supplementary volume of the Breitkopf

Complete Edition) that Schumann had sent to Wiedebein in 1828, an F major setting of Justinus Kerner's 'An Anna':

Nicht im Thale der süssen Heimath
Beim Gemurmel der Silberquelle
Bleich getragen aus dem Schlachtfeld
Denk' ich dein, du süsses Leben, denk ich dein.

(Not in the vale of the sweet homeland, by the murmur of the silver spring, do I think of thee, sweet life, but when carried, pallid from the field of battle.)

The ternary shape of the song is retained, also the move into the flattened submediant for the central section. In the piano version, however, Schumann more or less plunges into this new key instead of conventionally modulating, and there are one or two small melodic refinements as evidence of increasing maturity. The indication to the player is *senza passione ma espressivo*; its rapt intimacy drew very high praise from Liszt.

The last two movements were completely new, the scherzo as much Florestan's as the slow movement had been Eusebius's. The dotted rhythm and off-beat sforzandos of the recurrent F sharp minor *allegrissimo* section show the composer in uncommonly high spirits. In the first trio (*più allegro*) he begins to indulge in some characteristic rhythmic teasing so as to make third beats sound like accented first beats. In the much longer second trio, headed *Intermezzo: alla burla ma pomposo*, humour bubbles over. Here, the *Davidsbund* mercilessly caricature the Philistines, first in a kind of ceremonial polonaise, then in a passage of mock recitative ending on the wrong note (F natural instead of E).

In the finale, *allegro un poco maestoso*, Schumann's inexperience with larger forms is all too apparent. Certainly Eusebius makes some appealing contributions, but the subject-matter in general is episodically strung together in a curious sequence suggesting sonata form with the development section repeated after the normal recapitulation before a grandiose coda. This coda attempts to sum up the whole work: its backward glances at the first movement are subtle.

The Sonata is full of falling themes, some of them (especially in the first movement) far too indebted to the five-note Clara motto to be wholly coincidental. Yet it was not till the next work in F minor that Schumann wholly abandoned himself to – and openly acknowledged – the inspiration of these five notes.

SONATA IN F MINOR, OP. 14

The F minor Sonata was started in the autumn of 1835 and finished as a five-movement work, with two scherzi, in June 1836. Haslinger, the publisher, persuaded Schumann to remove both scherzi, and in November 1836 it appeared in print as a three-movement *Concert sans orchestre*. Schumann subsequently decided to restore the second scherzo (the first was published separately after his death), and in 1853 the work reappeared as the Piano Sonata no. 3, the G minor work having been issued in the meantime as no. 2. The dedication was to Moscheles, whose piano playing at Carlsbad in 1819 had made so deep an impression on the young Schumann that he had always wanted to write something for Moscheles in homage. (As we have seen, the *Allegro*, Op. 8, was the remains of one abandoned sonata attempt.) In the autumn of 1835 he had the added satisfaction of making Moscheles's personal acquaintance, and perhaps it was Moscheles's frank comment that the work 'did not fulfil the requirements of a concerto though it possessed the characteristic attributes of a grand sonata in the manner of Beethoven and Weber' that ultimately led Schumann to reform and rechristen it under a less misleading title.

In subject-matter, however, the Sonata is wholly Clara's. During its composition Schumann had faced up to the truth of his love for her, and had broken off his engagement to Ernestine, which would account for the music's tone of high romantic tumult. But more specifically, the slow movement is a set of variations on an 'Andantino de Clara Wieck' bringing her 'motto' theme, the falling figure of five notes, out into the open:

Ex. 9

This theme generates the greater part of the Sonata. Little else in Schumann's piano music is quite as monothematic as this work.

He declares his intentions, as it were, by using the five-note motif, in strong left-hand octaves, as the opening of the Sonata. In the eighth bar it is expanded in the treble as an impassioned melody, which after various subsidiary first-subject motifs and two rhythmically contrasted second subjects (all derivations of the Clara theme, either right way up or inverted) soars back in triumph in the relative major to crown the exposition. (He was to do much the same with the first subject in the first movement of his Piano Concerto several years later.) After so many ingenious transformations in the exposition, Schumann is hard pressed to find any further new light to shed on it in the central development section, which is brief and too much given to sequential repetition. Since this central development is the weakest section of the movement, it is strange to find it repeated after the normal recapitulation (the same plan favoured in the finale of the F sharp minor Sonata) before the imposing coda.

The rescued scherzo was the second of the original pair, based on the key of D flat. Its first four melody-notes are identical in pitch and time value (though not accentuation) with the melody in the second phrase of Clara's *andantino*; much else in the movement consists of falling-scale motifs or their inversions, all traceable to the same source. In the somewhat repetitive central trio section, marked by a drastic switch from five flats to three, then two, sharps, Schumann three times introduces an extended scale theme:

Ex. 10

Its second half is like some mature reincarnation of the 'hero going forth to his first battle' theme in *Papillons*. The whole phrase is a kind of heavenly reply to Clara's all too humdrum use of a similar melodic curve in her 'Ballet des revenants' (see p. 26 and Ex. 11).

Whether or not the shared motif *x* in each is the begetter of the beautiful B minor melody that plays so important a part in the *Davidsbündlertänze* can only remain a matter of surmise.

The third movement openly acknowledges Clara's plaintive *andantino*

Ex. 11

as the theme of its variations. It is the most overt reference so far made by Schumann to the five falling notes which in some way enshrined Clara's image for them both. It is a curious three-part theme, with each of its four-bar phrases repeated, the first over a reiterated tonic-dominant pedal, the second under a reiterated tonic-mediant chord, and the last ending inconclusively on the dominant. Schumann makes no attempt to follow up this pattern with any strictness, and in fact blossoms out freely enough in the last two of the four variations to explain why, perhaps, he headed the movement only *quasi*-variations. The postlude returns to the solemnity of Clara's dotted rhythmic motif, with nine reiterated chords of F minor by way of conclusion.

When revising the Sonata in 1853, Schumann changed the finale's original 6/16 time-signature into a simple 2/4 *prestissimo possibile*, incorporating two bars of the former in each one of the latter. Unhappily he did not attempt to tauten the argument itself, which if intended as sonata form with three subjects is a still more straggling example of his own favourite but wholly unsatisfactory variation of the classical pattern, i.e. with the development section repeated after the recapitulation proper, before the coda. The same recipe, in fact, as in the first movement of this sonata, and also the finale of Op. 11, in each case dissipating tension just at the moment when it most needs tautening.

Though the main theme incorporates a chromatically embellished version of Clara's motto, the thematic material in general is less distinguished than in the three earlier movements, with far more backward glances at the old virtuoso-variation-type note-spinning style that

Schumann was so anxious to renounce. Everything suggests that it was the finales of his sonatas that most betray the strain for Schumann, at this stage in his career, in filling large canvases.

SONATA IN G MINOR, OP. 22

Strictly speaking, the G minor Sonata should be dated 1828–38. Its slow movement grew from a song written when Schumann was eighteen, and the definitive finale was not added till he was twenty-eight. But it was most in his mind during 1833–5, the time when he made a frontal attack on sonata form, which always gave him so much more trouble than variations. Once again he went through all the usual agonies of self-doubt and self-criticism, some of which may be gleaned from a letter to Clara in March 1838:

> You are pretty right about the last movement of the sonata. It displeases me to such a degree (with the exception of certain passionate moments) that I have discarded it altogether. And I have come back to my original conception of the first movement, which you have not heard, but I am sure you will like.

The struggles were not in vain. As it now stands the work is more succinct than the F sharp minor and F minor sonatas, with a unity in the general conception once again deriving from the omni-presence of Clara's motto. His description of all his music at this time as 'one single cry of my heart for you in which your theme appears in every possible form' certainly embraces this G minor work.

The opening movement, *So rasch wie möglich*, brings a variant of the motto in the treble, and then imitatively in the bass, as the first subject. The motto then works its way into the chordal transition. It makes a substantial contribution to the second subject in the relative major, and reappears in inversion in the codetta. In the development Schumann allows himself the luxury of a new melody to relieve the somewhat mechanical pattern-making of the first subject treated in canonic imitation. Even so, he is soon in difficulties again, this time weakening the effect of the recapitulation with a twenty-four-bar anticipation of its G minor first subject. But by resisting the old temptation to repeat the development after a normal recapitulation, he tautens the argument, and further heightens the tension with a *più vivo* lead into a *noch schneller* coda – quite a problem for the performer in a movement already headed 'as fast as possible'. The succinctness of the subject-matter itself, in contrast to the straggling lyricism of the two other sonatas, also helps.

Like the slow movement of the F sharp minor sonata, that of the G minor work originated in the set of songs Schumann sent to Wiedebein for criticism in 1828. The words were Kerner's *Im Herbste*, and originally Schumann set them in E flat major in 2/4, emphasising their bittersweetness with a *Langsam und ausdrucksvoll* expression mark. In the Sonata the key is C major, the time-signature 6/8, and the heading *Andantino, getragen*. The whole movement is much more of a recomposition than was the case in the F sharp minor work. The song's second verse is embellished with flowing semiquavers, and there is a miniature development section mounting to an impassioned climax (with Clara's motto, both inverted and right way up, worked into the figuration) before the reprise and the characteristically beautiful coda.

The scherzo is the most condensed of all Schumann's essays in this form to date. The urgent G minor main theme itself is only twelve bars long. The two related episodes (full of typical syncopation) with which it alternates, last only eight and twenty-eight bars respectively, with repeats. The argument coheres the more closely by reason of the allpervasive falling motto in ingenious new shapes.

Though the definitive finale of 1838 is headed 'rondo', the form is nevertheless that compromise between rondo and sonata, not even definable as sonata-rondo, to which Schumann so frequently resorted in his sonatas. After the agitated G minor first subject and the suaver second in the relative major derived from Clara's motto-theme, there is a long episode of quasi-development with too much sequential patternmaking to stand up to recapitulation in full after the return of the first and second subjects in G minor and E flat major. To be fair, this movement is much more succinct than any of Schumann's previous experiments with the pattern. Yet the mechanical repetition (with adjustments of key) of the weakest part in the argument makes it difficult for the player to sustain tension right through to the last return of the agitated main theme before the breathless, whirlwind coda, aptly headed *prestissimo, quasi cadenza*. By the end of this sonata, too, the listener may feel his aural adventure has been too closely confined to G minor in the work as a whole.

The original finale of 1835 is an extended sonata-rondo, often lavishly ornate in figuration. It lacks the compression and economy for which Schumann seems to have been striving in this particular work, and from this point of view his displeasure with it is understandable. On the other hand its ideas are gloriously exuberant, and it teems with invention – both in the surreptitious references to Clara's motto (as in bars three and four in cross-rhythm) and in its general freshness of approach to a 6/16 time-signature and the variations of metrical unit obtainable from it. All in all, it is not difficult to understand why some pianists choose to substitute it for the later version, though since Schumann preferred the latter his wishes should be respected.

FANTASIA IN C, OP. 17

Schumann's first references to this work show that he envisaged it as a sonata. Excited by Liszt's schemes for raising money to build a monument to Beethoven at Bonn, he wrote at the end of 1836 to the publisher Kistner, explaining how he felt he could help:

> Florestan and Eusebius desire to contribute to Beethoven's monument and have written something for the purpose under the following title: *Ruins, Trophies, Palms. Grand Sonata for the Pianoforte for Beethoven's monument by* –. I have an idea as to how the work should be brought out, and have managed something very special, appropriate to the importance of the object. A black cover, or better still, binding, with gold ornamentation bearing in gold letters the words: *Obolus for Beethoven's monument.* On the chief title page palm-leaves might perhaps droop over the words of the top line. . . . The Sonata is in itself, too, sufficiently notable. The Adagio of the A major Symphony (Beethoven) is quoted in the Palms.

> Kistner, apparently, was less enthusiastic. The work was eventually published by Breitkopf and Härtel, not as a sonata but as a fantasia – perhaps in view of its unconventional sequence of movements. The descriptive titles were removed, and only through the dedication to Liszt did Schumann make any outward reference to his intended tribute to Beethoven. But that he was trying to communicate something beyond the actual notes was clear from the Schlegel quotation which he wrote at the head of the score:

> Durch alle Töne tönet
> Im bunten Erdentraum
> Ein leiser Ton gezogen
> Für den, der heimlich lauschet.

(Through all the sounds in earth's motley dream, one soft note can be heard by him who listens stealthily.)

As so often, more intimate clues were given to Clara when the work was finished in 1838:

> I have besides finished a Fantasie in three movements, which I had sketched out, all but the details, in June 1836. I think the first movement is more impassioned than anything I have ever written – a deep lament for you [17 March 1838]. The next things to be printed are some fantasias, but to distinguish them from the *Phantasie-Stücke* I have called them 'Ruins', 'Triumphal Arch' and 'Constellation' [13 April 1838]. Tell me what you think of the *Fantasie*. Does it not conjure up many images in your mind? I like this melody best {see Ex. 16}. I suppose you are the 'note' in the motto? I almost think you must be [9 June 1839].

It is important to remember that when Schumann started the work, Clara's father had forbidden the two by now openly declared lovers to meet or correspond. Music was their only means of communication. And Schumann's way of laying bare his heart to Clara in the passionate first movement was one of the most subtle on which he had yet stumbled; it also explains why he had chosen this particular work for his intended homage to Beethoven. Running through the entire movement there are veiled allusions to a theme which in the coda he at last states quite openly:

Ex. 12

Its kinship with the main theme of the sixth of Beethoven's *An die ferne Geliebte* songs is too close to be anything other than deliberate, especially in view of words such as:

> Take them, then, these songs I sang thee,
> Songs of passion, songs of pain.
> Let them like an echo tender
> All our love call back again.

Ex. 13

Nimm sie hin denn, die - se Lie · der

35

The urgency of Schumann's emotion overcame all those formal problems that had dogged him before in larger canvases. Though headed 'Fantastic and passionate throughout', and very flexible indeed in pulse, the first movement is nevertheless the most masterly of all his keyboard arguments in sonata form. The ideas, all vintage Schumann, merge into each other without visible seams, as do the larger sections. The first subject is perhaps the most beautiful version of the Clara motto that he had yet devised:

Ex. 14

And imperceptibly it melts into the movement's first reference to the *An die ferne Geliebte* theme:

Ex. 15

'The melody I like best' which Schumann quoted in his letter of June 1839 is a short phrase:

Ex. 16

growing out of the second subject, which in its turn is artfully evolved from both Clara's theme and the Beethoven quotation. The exposition is not repeated. In the course of the development there is a striking transformation of the second subject's initial uprising fourth in a grave C minor episode headed *Im Legendenton*, and almost immediately afterwards a very pointed reference to the Beethoven quotation, though here made to sound much more disturbed. The movement's crowning glory is nevertheless the coda, with its profoundly eloquent declaration of love through Beethoven's song. This time the meaning is unmistakable. Its C major glow affirms that Schumann's own hopes were not entirely in ruins, despite his original title for the movement.

'Trophies' and 'Triumphal Arch' were both considered as titles for the second movement, where Schumann moves from C major to E flat, Beethoven's most heroic key. The movement is a sonata-rondo bound together by a proud march-like theme to which Schumann could easily have sent out the *Davidsbund* for a further assault on the Philistines. The dotted rhythm of the first episode suggests the *alla marcia* of Beethoven's A major Sonata, Op. 101, as a possible influence. The falling notes of Clara's motto are worked into the texture in canon here, and again in the continuation of the central episode in A flat major. The opening of this central *Etwas langsamer* is quintessentially Schumannesque (at this period) in presenting the tune in an off-beat version which needs to be seen as well as heard for its full subtlety to emerge. Equally characteristic is his fondness for melody in inner voices instead of always at the top. As he once put it in a letter to Clara, 'You know how I often use strange middle parts – these are my sign-manual'. The *molto più mosso* coda shows Schumann exulting in keyboard virtuosity as he was not often to do again.

The slow movement, variously entitled 'Palms', 'Starry Crown', 'Constellation', comes last, like a profound benediction. Nothing in the earlier sonatas, or indeed any of his previous works, springs from such deep places of the heart. Clara's motto-theme is introduced in the bass as early as the fifth bar, supporting a new melody characteristically sung in the lower part of the right hand and then echoed at the octave in the triplet figuration. A surprise switch from C to A flat major brings a new theme (*etwas bewegter*) which Schumann had noted in his sketchbook on 30 November 1836, with the words 'dabei selig geschwärmt' (was in blissful rapture). Clara's theme even weaves its way into this as it works towards a fervent F major chordal climax. Recapitulation follows without development. The coda grows from the *etwas bewegter* theme; it brings one last exultant surge of emotion, using a startling chord sequence akin to that of the introduction, before sinking to rest in a radiant C major.[1]

DAVIDSBÜNDLERTÄNZE, OP. 6

The *Davidsbündlertänze* grew from the autumn of 1837, a bitter-sweet year for Schumann, beginning with almost total estrangement from Clara, but which on 14 August, known as Eusebius's day in the Saxon calendar, brought their secret engagement, regardless of parental disapproval.

Schumann's state of mind when putting pen to paper is perhaps best reflected in the old rhyme prefixed to his first edition:

> In 'all und jeder Zeit
> Verknüpft sich Lust und Leid,
> Bleibt fromm in Lust und seid
> Beim Leid mit Mut bereit.

(Along the way we go are mingled weal and woe; in weal, though glad, be grave, in woe, though sad, be brave.)

All eighteen pieces were initialled with an F or E (four times the two appear together) as clue to their character. Over the ninth he wrote, 'Here Florestan kept silent, but his lips were quivering with emotion.' The last of all was inscribed, 'Quite superfluously Eusebius remarked as follows, but all the time great joy spoke from his eyes.' In Schumann's second edition of 1851 he suppressed all extraneous clues of this nature, besides the *Tänze* in the title and a few fanciful performing indications in German, as well as making one or two small and mostly unimportant text revisions.

Characteristically, the most revealing information was reserved for Clara in their correspondence:

> There are many bridal thoughts in the dances, which were suggested by the most delicious excitement that I ever remember. I will explain them all to you one day [5 January 1838. And a few days later,] Have

1 A manuscript of the *Fantasia* (recently discovered in the National Széchényi Library in Budapest), carrying Schumann's signature and the date 19 December 1838, reveals that he originally intended to end the work by recalling the *An die ferne Geliebte* quotation – with a small but significant change of one melody note and its harmonisation.

you not received the *Davidstänze* (one copy is in silver print)? I sent them to you last Saturday week. You might patronise them a little, do you hear? They are my particular property. But my Clara will understand all that is contained in the dances, for they are dedicated to her, and that more emphatically than any of my other things. The whole story is a *Polterabend*, and now you can imagine it all from the beginning to the end. If ever I was happy at the piano it was when I was composing those [a few days later].

In spite of Schumann's references to a *Polterabend*, in German folklore the 'wedding eve when all sorts of mischievous hobgoblins and sprites torment the bride with hilarious practical jokes', Clara's response suggests that without her lover at her side to enlighten her she did not immediately 'understand all that was contained in the dances'.

However dampened by this in secret, Schumann at least replied discreetly:

You pass over the *Davidsbündlertänze* very lightly. I think they are quite different from the *Carnaval*, compared with which they are what a face is to a mask. But I may be mistaken, as I have not forgotten them yet. All I know is that they were written in happiness, and the others in toil and sorrow [March 1838].

That 'written in happiness' is borne out by the spontaneity of the *Davidsbündlertänze*, in contrast to the laborious reincarnations and revisions of most of Schumann's earlier works. No trial sketches exist. His 'as a face is to a mask' is fair comment, too, in comparing the dances with *Carnaval* (together with *Papillons*, their nearest counterparts): the pieces are not merely pretty conceits, but were written with his heart's blood. But the secrets of the music are buried deeper than in *Carnaval*.

The one overt musical clue comes at the start, where the opening two bars are inscribed 'Motto von C.W.' Schumann immediately carries the motto into the relative minor, in inversion, possibly to symbolise the 'weal and woe' of the epigraph:

Ex. 17

Motto von C.W.

The motto is in fact the opening of a mazurka from Clara's *Soirées musicales*, Op. 6, which Schumann had reviewed in the *Neue Zeitschrift* shortly before starting the *Davidsbündlertänze*. Its own falling seconds, either as seconds or expanded into longer flights, contribute almost enough in themselves for the work to rank as yet another variant of Schumann's favourite variation form. Yet it soon becomes plain that this motto is not the only source-material. After Eusebius's tenderly poignant B minor extension of the motto (no. 2, *Innig*), Florestan's exuberant no. 3 in G (*Mit Humor. Etwas hahnebüchen* – 'rather heavy-handed') makes a host of other allusions as soon as it has shot its opening bolt in the form of a joyous, uprising extension of the 'C.W.' phrase. The inescapable five-note falling figure reappears in the bass at the eighth bar (actually the self-same notes are introduced in the tune in bars 2–3 of the preceding number). In the seventeenth bar there is an unmistakable reference, albeit in fractured rhythm, to the 'hero going forth to his first battle' theme from the start of *Papillons*, subsequently quoted in *Carnaval*:

Ex. 18

And at bar 55 there is an undisguised reference to the main refrain of 'Promenade' in *Carnaval*. Most important of all, however, is the motif surreptitiously worked into the bass in the brief recapitulation:

Ex. 19

This theme is yet more insistent in Florestan's no. 4 in B minor (*Ungeduldig*), though still kept to the bass. It re-emerges in Eusebius's no. 5 in D (*Einfach*), then again transposed into G minor in his no. 7 (*Nicht schnell. Mit äusserst starker Empfindung*), and most appealingly of all, in no. 11 in B minor (*Einfach*), where it is brought right out into the open as the melody:

Ex. 20 (i) No. 4

(ii) No. 5   (iii) No. 7

(iv) No. 11

Though as integral a part of the suite as Clara's opening motto, Schumann kept this theme's personal significance his own secret. Roger Fiske has suggested that it might be a reference to the central tune of Clara's 'Ballet des revenants' from her *Quatre Pièces caractéristiques*, Op. 5 (Ex. 11). Eric Sams regards it as a kind of retrograde transposition of an enciphered form of Clara's name. Shorn of the opening B natural, as in Ex. 20 (ii), it could just as well be a simple inverted variant of the falling five-note motto running through all the music of this period. Whatever it is, it is of vital importance throughout, not least in veiled allusions such as the trio of no. 16.

Some of the dances grow more from free-ranging *Polterabend* fancies than from any of the work's basic musical themes. For instance in the course of no. 13 in B minor-major, headed *Wild und lustig*, Eusebius seems to calm an agitated Florestan with the strains of a wedding chorale played on an organ. But the main motifs are never long forgotten, albeit sometimes transformed out of all immediate recognition, such as the rapturous E flat major blossoming of the 'C.W.' motto through Eusebius's eyes amidst typical impatience from Florestan in no. 15 in B flat (*Frisch*). One of the work's master-strokes of unification is the recall of Eusebius's poignant B minor variation (no. 2) after the blissful opening of no. 17 in B major, headed 'Wie aus der Ferne' (As if from a distance), and the fact that Schumann wrote these words in the score suggests very strongly that this opening tune might have originated somewhere or other in one of Clara's own works (cf. 'Stimme aus der Ferne' in the last of the *Novelletten*: see p. 52).

Originally the eighteen dances were published in two sets. The first nine travel from G major through B minor, G major, B minor, D major, D minor, G minor and C minor to C major; the second nine move from

D minor through D major, E minor, B minor-major, E flat major, B flat major, G major-B minor and B major-minor and again back to C major. B minor can be seen as an important centre in this subtle tonal scheme, and C major is significantly reserved for nos. 9 and 18 alone, where, as the original inscriptions revealed, Florestan and Eusebius speak directly to Clara of their fears and hopes. In no. 9 Florestan quivers with pained emotion in an excitably indignant dotted version of the motto, interspersed with echoes of his own battling hero theme. And transformed into a simple, inward waltz, the falling seconds of Clara's motto embody all the wonder of Eusebius's joy in no. 18 before the clock chimes midnight and the vision fades into the darkness of the night.

KREISLERIANA, OP. 16

Kreisleriana, subtitled 'Fantasien', also came into being in a spontaneous flood: it was completed in four days during April 1838. In a letter the following year to Simonin de Sire, a Belgian acquaintance, Schumann explained its name:

> The title conveys nothing to any but Germans. Kreisler is one of E. T. A. Hoffmann's creations, an eccentric, wild and witty conductor.

His special interest in the character derived from his belief that Hoffmann's model was Ludwig Böhner (1787–1860), a real-life musical eccentric whom he described at length in a letter to Baron von Fricken in September 1834:

> The latest and most important event is that old Ludwig Böhner gave a concert here yesterday. I suppose you are aware that in his palmy days he was as celebrated as Beethoven, and was the original of Hoffmann's Kapellmeister Kreisler. But he looked so poverty-stricken that it quite depressed me. He was like an old lion with a thorn in his foot. The day before yesterday, he improvised at my house for a few hours; the old fire flashed out now and again, but on the whole it was very gloomy and dull. His former life is now avenging itself. He used to jeer at the world with infinite boldness and arrogance, and now the tables are turned upon him. If I had time, I should like one day to write 'Böhneriana' for our paper, as I have heard a great deal about him from his own lips. His life contains so much that is both humorous and pathetic.

How much of this projected verbal 'Böhneriana' went into the musical *Kreisleriana* is a moot point. Many were the days, weeks and months when Schumann saw his own life as nothing but a tale of thwarted dreams: in this sense sympathy for Kreisler was inevitable. Yet Wasielewski was probably right in claiming that the music could just as easily have been called *Wertheriana* or *Schumanniana*: everything suggests that strong personal feeling lies below the literary cloak. Again, letters to Clara provide the clearest pointer:

> Play my *Kreisleriana* often. A positively wild love is in some of the movements, and your life and mine, and the way you look.

The earliest reference to it (13 April 1838) goes even further:

> How full of music I am now, and always such lovely melodies! Only fancy, since my last letter I have finished another whole book of new things. You and one of your ideas are the principal subject, and I shall call them *Kreisleriana* and dedicate them to you; yes, to you, and to nobody else; and you will smile so sweetly when you see yourself in them. Even to myself my music now seems wonderfully intricate in spite of its simplicity; its eloquence comes straight from the heart.

The suggestion here is that the music not only enshrines Clara's image during their aching separation, but is also based on some secret, underlying 'master' theme either by her, or else symbolising her in his mind – such as an extension of the B E D A motto found at the end of his bitter article, 'The Editor's Ball', published in 1837, in which this name enshrined the girl he still loved as opposed to Ambrosia (her other self) who seemed to be flirting with a rival suitor.

Ex. 21

It is surprising how much of the essence of *Kreisleriana* that brief motif seems to contain. The eventual dedication nevertheless was not to Clara but to Chopin. A second edition some twelve years later brought only very small textual revisions, including a conclusive ending in G minor to no. 5 which is not an improvement on the original end on the dominant.

No matter what the precise thematic source, there is an unmistakable inner unity in *Kreisleriana*. The eight pieces must be played in sequence, as a complete whole. Though the starting point is D minor, the true tonal pivot is G minor/B flat major. The restlessly searching G minor numbers belong to Florestan as clearly as the idyllic B flat major ones do to Eusebius, even though in this work there are no names or initials. Whatever the key, most of the pieces push chromaticism to a point never previously explored by Schumann: this, perhaps more than any other single factor, gives *Kreisleriana* its special aura of introspective intensity, of tortuous and often tortured soul-searching. The 'simplicity' to which Schumann referred in his letter to Clara applies only to the fact that the suite makes no virtuoso demands: in every other respect the music is 'wonderfully intricate'. This example from no. 2 makes it easy to appreciate Clara's plea that he should be more lucid, as it hurt her so much when people did not understand him:

Ex. 22

That passage also typifies Schumann's increased interest in linear texture. The influence of Schubert and the dance-floor, once so potent, cedes to something much more baroque, albeit romanticised baroque.

The form of most of the pieces is ternary, or simple rondo, with contrasting (yet also subtly related) episodes to relieve obsessive rhythms or patterns. Though the falling five-note figure is not wholly forgotten, as nos. 1 and 5 make particularly clear, a three-note motif, mostly ascending but sometimes in inversion too, emerges as another potent seminal force throughout this particular work. The first number has certain affinities with the rejected finale of the G minor Sonata. And Schumann reverted to the main theme of the whimsical no. 8 in the finale (originally entitled 'Spring's Farewell') of his 'Spring' Symphony three years later. The ending is a very characteristic fading away into distant silence, again in the depths of the piano, as in the *Davidsbündlertänze*.

End of a Chapter

In 1840, the year of his marriage, Schumann temporarily abandoned the solo piano is favour of song. But before the break, he brought his miraculous first decade as a keyboard composer to a head with a great outpouring of miniatures, mostly grouped under collective titles: *Fantasiestücke, Kinderscenen, Novelletten, Klavierstücke, Nachtstücke, Drei Romanzen*. The exceptions are the *Arabeske, Blumenstück* and *Humoreske*, all three separate, self-contained pieces, also *Faschingsschwank aus Wien*, which in a sense is a reversion to the suite-like thinking oï his middle 'Florestan and Eusebius' period, albeit without quite so close an inner unity. Each group of pieces of these last pre-wedding years has some recognisable character of its own to justify its collective title. Yet individual pieces can be detached for separate performance in a way inconceivable with, say, the constituent parts of *Davidsbündlertänze* or *Kreisleriana*. This was Schumann's heyday in the sphere of the short character-piece, each one over in a matter of minutes, yet as potent in mood evocation as anything in the whole literature of the piano.

FANTASIESTÜCKE, OP. 12

The *Fantasiestücke* were written in the spring and early summer of 1837, and were published by Breitkopf and Härtel the following February. The dedication is to Anna Robena Laidlaw, a young pianist-visitor to Leipzig, who sufficiently cared for Schumann to give him a lock of her hair when she left. All eight pieces in the set have descriptive titles,[1] though again here, as so often, Schumann insisted in letters to friends that he added them after completing the music, that the music itself suggested them. No matter which way round, these titles are extraordinarily apt, and invaluable clues in interpretation. Schumann was well aware that these pieces were more direct, less enigmatic, than much he had recently produced. In December 1837 he wrote to Clara:

> None of my things will really do for playing in public, but among the *Fantasiestücke* there is one, *In der Nacht*, and another *Traumeswirren*; they will be out soon, so just look at them.

Apart from their evocative poetry, the *Fantasiestücke* also reveal Schumann's craftsmanship at its most consummate. *Des Abends* (At evening)

1   A ninth, first published in the *Schweizerische Musikzeitung*, December 1935, is headed only by three asterisks.

is quintessentially Schumannesque in rhythm, texture and key. The melody flows in triple rhythm across a 2/8 time-signature (duple and triple cross-currents had a lifelong fascination for him). The tune is an integral part of the surrounding texture, sometimes woven right inside it. Changes of key are enharmonic and swift, with startling juxta-positions of the five flats of D flat major and the four sharps of E major. The exhilaration of *Aufschwung* (Soaring) and the caprice of *Grillen* (Whims) are canalised within the disciplined banks of sonata-rondo form. Between them comes the intimately eloquent, monothematic *Warum?* (Why?), with all its questioning evolved from the four-bar opening phrase. Though Schumann sometimes feared that *In der Nacht* (In the night) was too long, it was nevertheless his favourite because, as he wrote to Clara:

> After I had finished it I found, to my delight, that it contained the story of Hero and Leander. Of course you know it, how Leander swam every night through the sea to his love, who awaited him at the beacon, and showed him the way with lighted torch. When I am playing *Die Nacht* I can't get rid of the idea. First he throws himself into the sea; she calls him, he answers; he battles with the waves, and reaches land in safety. Then the cantilena, when they are clasped in one another's arms, until they have to part again and he can't tear himself away, until night wraps everything in darkness once more. Do tell me if the music suggests the same things to you.

The melodic motives, as they expand, do in fact rise and fall like waves, and enharmonic modulation, again as in *Des Abends*, makes the key colouring richly kaleidoscopic. After *Fabel*, with its *presto* adventures enclosed within a recurrent, slow 'once upon a time' refrain, *Traumes-Wirren* (Dream Confusion) introduces a note of light-fingered, almost Chopinesque virtuosity. For the slower middle section, Schumann plunges from F major into D flat major, from there embarking on a false start to the recapitulation in G flat major before eventually resuming the F major whirls. As for *Ende vom Lied* (End of the song), Schumann's own explanation to Clara is probably the best:

> Towards the end everything gives place to a gay wedding, but then the sorrow about you returned, and one hears the marriage bells and death knell sounding together.

There is certainly no mistaking the falling five-note Clara motif towards the end of the subdued, chordal coda.

KINDERSCENEN, OP. 15

Music for the young to play came later in Schumann's output, when he had children of his own. Despite technical simplicity, the thirteen pieces of *Kinderscenen* are an adult's recollections of childhood, for adult performers. The best description, as so often, is his own, in a letter to Clara of March 1838:

> I have found out that nothing sharpens one's imagination so much as to be expecting and longing for something, and this has been my case for the last few days. I have been waiting for your letter, and consequently have composed book-fulls of things – wonderful, crazy, and solemn stuff; you will open your eyes when you come to play it. In fact, sometimes I feel simply bursting with music. But before I forget it, let me tell you what else I have composed. Whether it was an echo of what you said to me once, 'that sometimes I seemed to you like a child', anyhow, I suddenly got an inspiration, and knocked off about thirty quaint little things, from which I have selected twelve [sic] and called them *Kinderscenen*. They will amuse you, but of course you must forget that you are a performer. They have such titles as *Fürchtenmachen*, *Am Kamin*, *Haschemann*, *Bittendes Kind*, *Ritter vom Steckenpferd*, *Von fremden Ländern*, *Curiose Geschichte*, etc., and I don't know what besides. Well, they all explain themselves, and what's more are as easy as possible.

It would be difficult to point to a redundant note in any of these pieces. In their unassuming way, they are even more remarkable than the *Fantasiestücke* in distilling a poetic idea into its purest, simplest and most potent form. Nor does their very close unity as a set merely reside in the theme of childhood. Nearly all the pieces seem to grow from the thematic contour of the opening of *Von fremden Ländern und Menschen* (About foreign lands and peoples), though often with the first note omitted, leaving a four-note falling figure instead of the complete Clara motif:

Ex. 23

As so often, Schumann insisted that he added the titles afterwards. Nevertheless the connection between subject and notes could scarcely be closer. The entreaties of *Bittendes Kind* (Pleading child) are left un-appeased on an unresolved dominant seventh, just as sleep overtakes the child of *Kind im Einschlummern* (Child going to sleep) on the sub-dominant chord. Plunges from D into F major heighten the happiness of *Glückes genug* (Lots of happiness), while the choice of the searching key of G sharp minor intensifies the seriousness of *Fast zu ernst* (Almost too serious). *Träumerei* (Reverie), with a whole world of aspiration compressed within the rise and fall of its opening four-bar phrase, is as much a monothematic miracle as *Warum?* in Op. 12. Sudden tempo changes and unexpected sforzandos emphasise the eeriness of *Fürchten-machen* (Frightening). *Der Dichter spricht* (The poet speaks) is a typical Schumannesque epilogue, of the kind he so often favoured in his songs and song-cycles, fading away into characteristic distance and silence.

ARABESKE, OP. 18; BLUMENSTÜCK, OP. 19; HUMORESKE, OP. 20

The *Arabeske* (1838), *Blumenstück* (1839) and *Humoreske* (1839) stand in a category apart in that none is part of a set. In all three Schumann favours sectional construction rather than any kind of continuous development, in which respect they are akin to the *Novelletten*, though the thought sequence is quite different in each. In a letter to Clara of January 1839 he comments:

> I have finished variations, but not upon any theme, and in *Guirlande*, as I am going to call it, everything is interwoven in such a peculiar way.

Ambiguous, perhaps, yet just some small clue as to the way his mind was working at this time.

The *Arabeske* is in simple rondo form, its main C major theme in flowing semiquavers alternating with slightly slower episodes marked Minore I (E minor) and Minore II (A minor). Yet even this charming drawing-room aquarelle has the distinguishing Schumann touch in the ruminative episode (built from what is surely another reference to the Clara motif), leading to the first return of the main theme, then again in the *lento* commentary on that same episode which serves as coda – in which Schumann extracts almost as much eloquence from the key of C as in his great C major *Fantasia*, Op. 17.

The *Blumenstück* is more easily recognisable as 'variations but not upon any theme', and certainly could just as well have been entitled *Guirlande*. Short, closely related sections are strung together in a sequence precisely indicated in the score under the numbers I II III II IV

V Minore II IV II, followed by a short coda. The tonality is firmly anchored to D flat, despite excursions into closely related flat keys – and one startling enharmonic lunge from A flat into E major in the course of II (the section which Schumann chooses to vary slightly on each return). Since the same figuration (i.e. melody note alternating with off-beat accompaniment woven into a continuous semiquaver web) persists throughout every section, the effect for the ear alone can prove a bit monotonous. Yet closer investigation of the score reveals subtler thinking than might be apparent at first hearing. The piece could even be considered as variations not upon a theme but a motto: the Clara motif is incorporated into every section (though less obviously in IV and V) after presentation in various guises in I.

The *Humoreske* is not only the longest and most complex in construction, but also the most personal. Schumann recognised it as the most important of the three:

> I have been all the week at the piano, composing, writing, laughing and crying, all at once. You will find this state of things nicely described in my Op. 20, the *Grosse Humoreske* . . . twelve sheets composed in a week.

Writing to his Belgian acquaintance, Simonin de Sire, he enlarged on his choice of title:

> Neither does *Humoreske* convey anything in French. It is a pity that no good and apt words exist in the French language for those two most characteristic and deeply rooted of German conceptions, *das Gemütliche* (*Schwärmerische*) and *Humor*, the latter of which is a happy combination of *Gemütlichkeit* and wit.

To his old friend, Henriette Voigt, he admitted that the content was more melancholy than humorous.

The work is in fact a sequence of mood pictures, interwoven in a very 'peculiar way' (to borrow Schumann's phrase), yet somehow so effortlessly cohering as to suggest they might have been conceived as variations in search of a theme, or even as variations on some secret, unstated master-theme existing only in Schumann's mind. The most important sections are in themselves planned in a kind of self-contained ternary form, with a few surreptitious cross-references. Nevertheless the real unity seems to lie at a rather deeper level than related note-patterns. However daring the passing chords and modulations, the main sections do not stray beyond the dominant and relative minor (and their own dominant and subdominant relations) of the basic key of B flat. As regards the texture and figuration, it is almost a compendium of all that is most characteristic of the composer in middle life (after the accident which stopped his virtuoso career), even down to a mysterious 'inner voice' on an extra middle stave. One of the more lyrical sections carries the significant word *Innig* above it as proof of Schumann's very deep involvement.

NOVELLETTEN, OP. 21

The *Novelletten*, dedicated to Adolph Henselt, are the most extended of the 1838 collections. Schumann gave no individual descriptive titles to the eight pieces, but generalised about them quite a lot. 'Longish, connected adventure stories' were his words to Fischhof (April 1838). To Hirschbach he subsequently commented that they were 'closely connected, were written with great enjoyment, and are on the whole light and superficial, excepting one or two sections where I go deeper'. The most personal explanations were nevertheless reserved for Clara. In a letter of 6 February 1838, he wrote that during the last three weeks

> I have composed a shocking amount for you, jests, Egmont stories, family scenes with fathers, a wedding – and called the whole *Novelletten*.

In 1839, when publication was imminent, he confessed to her:

> In the *Novelletten* you, my bride, appear in every possible setting and circumstance, and in other ways in which you are irresistible! Yes, only look at me! I assert that he alone can write *Novelletten* who knows eyes like yours, who has touched such lips as yours – in short it may well be possible to do better work, but hardly to do anything similar.

Even to his old teacher, Dorn, in September 1839 he cited the *Novelletten* as one of the five works almost entirely inspired by his beloved.

The Clara link is most clear in the last, also the longest and most self-determining in form – though Kathleen Dale has neatly summarised it as a pair of scherzos each with its own two trios.[1] What in fact holds the piece together is the minim melody that eventually surfaces, with deepening emotion, from the lively dotted rhythm of the second trio. Marked *Stimme aus der Ferne* (voice from afar), this is a direct quotation (with the same harmonies though in different key and

[1] In Gerald Abraham, *Schumann: a Symposium* (London 1952), p. 57.

VIER CLAVIERSTÜCKE, OP. 32

The *Scherzo, Gigue* and *Romanze* of Op. 32 were written in 1838 and the *Fughetta* in 1839. The *Gigue* and *Fughetta*, both in G minor, in fact appeared in print separately before Schumann eventually decided to publish the four pieces as a group. With the *Scherzo* embarking from B flat major and the *Romanze* cast in D minor (the relative major and dominant minor, respectively, of G minor) the key-scheme certainly encourages performance as a set. In style, however, these four pieces are not quite as homogeneous as Schumann's other collections of this period, unless a predilection for dotted rhythm can be accepted as a unifying factor.

In the *Scherzo*, the dotted motif even makes its way into the smoother central trio section in D minor. The *Gigue* starts off as a three-part fugue, and makes a feature of contrapuntal imitation throughout. Yet the cut of the material remains Schumannesque. The *Romanze* is demonstratively ardent: the main section is even headed 'very fast and with bravura'. But the middle section melts into the relative major, slower tempo and a glorious, characteristic melody which could even be considered yet another variation of the five-note motto. The *Fughetta*, with its whimsical subject harmonised from the start, is again (like the *Gigue*) no more classical than Mendelssohn (who could well have already turned Schumann's mind in this direction) despite its impressive organ-loft type ending complete with Picardy third.

FASCHINGSSCHWANK AUS WIEN, OP. 26

Money, or rather the lack of it, was one of the main reasons why Friedrich Wieck so doggedly fought Schumann's proposed marriage to Clara: for his daughter Wieck wanted immediate, not posthumous, grandeur. Accordingly during the winter of 1838–9 Schumann went off to Vienna to investigate prospects for publishing the *Neue Zeitschrift für Musik* in that city, and generally making a more remunerative career for himself there. In the event he was disappointed, though as he put it, 'An artist cannot fail, however, to derive stimulus and benefit from the city of Vienna, and I have written a good deal though not of my best.' Many of the smaller pieces just discussed grew from this background, though inevitably, by reason of its title, the visit is chiefly remembered by *Faschingsschwank aus Wien* (Carnival jest from Vienna). Only the finale was added after Schumann's return to Leipzig; publication eventually followed in 1841.

The title itself was a kind of salvage operation: the first choice for *Carnaval* had been *Fasching: Schwänke auf vier Noten*. To Simonin de Sire, the eventual dedicatee of Op. 26, he described it as 'a great romantic sonata'. On another occasion he used the phrase 'ein romantisches Schaustück' – a romantic showpiece. The 'jest' of the title is thought to refer primarily to the disguised quotation of the *Marseillaise*, then forbidden in Vienna, in the course of the first movement. (Schumann quoted it in three later works.) For this opening *allegro* Schumann again uses an extended, ritornello-type construction, with an exuberant 24-bar theme in B flat major as the connecting link. Gerald Abraham has suggested[1] that several masked *Davidsbund* members lurk behind the contrasting episodes: Chopin and Mendelssohn in the two in G minor and Schubert in that in F sharp. By the same token it would be easy to identify the second E flat major episode with Beethoven in view of its kinship with the trio of the minuetto of his Sonata in E flat, Op. 31, no. 3. The first E flat episode (referred to again in the coda) could also well represent Schumann himself, since he so much loved to tease his listeners with syncopation making triple time into duple. (The melodic contour at the outset also awakens memories of the coda to the penultimate number of *Kreisleriana*.)

In the plaintive falling phrases of the G minor *Romanze*, Schumann seems to pine for his distant beloved again, though a short-cut modulation into C major, then G, brings a brief upsurge of new hope in the middle section. The surprise turning at the end also suggests that all is not lost.

In the *Scherzino*, a miniature rondo in B flat, Schumann frolics with a dotted rhythm that might have sounded obsessive but for his startling switches of key. An enharmonically changed D flat brings the main theme back in A major, before consecutive dominant sevenths built up on E and F restore the home key. He makes equal sport out of unpredictable dominant sevenths, in minims, nearer the end.

The surging *Intermezzo* in E flat minor is the most passionately involved of the five movements: Schumann rarely used such complex keys without something very personal to say. He could have called it a song without words. Both the shape of the melody, with its recurrent reiterated quavers, and the layout of the accompaniment, which in itself would be quite enough to keep both hands busy, suggest that he had some romantic verse in his mind as he wrote. The movement is remarkably prophetic of 1840 and its great outpouring of song.

[1] *Op. cit.*, p. 48.

After several years' neglect of sonata-form, Schumann reverts to it in the *vivacissimo* finale in B flat – as if to justify his description of the work as 'a great romantic sonata'. The argument is much more concise than anything he had achieved before in this form: there is no recapitulated development, for instance. Yet the sequence of events and the figuration are all a bit too self-consciously patterned to suggest that he had really made this form his servant. As a pianistic *tour de force* it can nevertheless prove brilliantly effective, not least the characteristic *presto* coda.

Marriage and its Aftermath

Until 1840, the year of his marriage, Schumann had little thought for anything but music for his own and Clara's instrument. Throughout his remaining years he never lost interest in the piano in collaboration with the voice, in chamber works, and with orchestra, but solo music for this instrument now took a secondary role. Nevertheless in 1845, perhaps to relax from the nervous exhaustion of more ambitious orchestral and choral undertakings, he returned to the piano to write fugues, also contrapuntal *Studies* and *Sketches* for the then fashionable pedal-piano. Soon afterwards his own growing family turned his thoughts to music for the young to play. Subsequently he salvaged a great number of discarded pieces from all periods of his life for publication in two substantial collections. He even produced several more sets of related miniatures akin to those which immediately preceded his marriage.

THE CONTRAPUNTAL MUSIC

'I shall never get on with Dorn: he wants to persuade me that music is nothing but fugues,' wrote Schumann to Clara in 1832, of even his most enlightened teacher. In youth he jokingly claimed Jean Paul as his only real mentor in counterpoint, and all his strokes of contrapuntal ingenuity as things he noticed only after they were written. Love of Bach soon modified this rebellious attitude, as his notebooks of the later 1830s make very clear. Yet it was not till after his marriage, when he turned to large-scale symphonies, chamber works, oratorios and dramatic music (which could not always be worked out through his own ten fingers at the keyboard) that the *lacunae* of his early training were really brought home to him, not least in comparison with the exceptionally polished craftsmanship of his admired friend, Mendelssohn. Accordingly, after a crisis of nervous exhaustion in 1844 induced by his *Faust* music, he started 1845 in a mood of determination to strengthen his counterpoint through a renewed study of Bach, and with Cherubini's *Cours de Contrepoint* never too far out of reach either. Clara, of course, joined in. On 23 January her diary records:

> Today we began to study counterpoint, which, in spite of the labour, gave me great pleasure, for I saw – what I had never thought to see – a fugue of my own, and then several others, for we continue our studies regularly every day. . . . He himself has been seized by a regular passion for fugues, and beautiful themes pour from him.

As for Schumann, he subsequently confessed, 'From 1845 onwards, when I started to invent and work out in my head, a quite different way of composing began to develop.'

The first fruits were the *Four Fugues*, Op. 72, of which nos. 1 and 2 were already completed by February and March. All four are rather too persistently thematic, but succinctly so, and contain examples of augmentation (the bass at the end of no. 2 is a telling example of this), inversion, and stretto startlingly indicative of the craftsman Schumann could have become, given a normal studentship in youth. But while all four subjects have very positive musical character, only into that of no. 3 in F minor did Schumann also manage to write his own initials – despite its resemblance to the opening of Chopin's F minor study (from the *Trois nouvelles études*). Headed *Nicht schnell und sehr ausdrucksvoll* (not fast and very expressive), this chromatic fugue shows Schumann really making the form his own (note the dramatic hiatus fourteen bars before the end), generating some harmonic tension, and generally justifying his original intention of calling the set *Vier Charakterfugen*.

Again it is Clara's diary that explains what followed:

> On 24 April we received a pedal for our piano, on hire, which gave us great pleasure. The chief object was to enable us to practise for the organ. [The pedal-piano had just been introduced into the Leipzig Music School, where Schumann had taught composition since 1843, for the organ scholars' practice.] Robert, however, soon found a greater interest in this instrument, and composed several sketches and studies for pedal-piano, which will certainly make a great sensation, being something entirely new.

The most erudite of these pieces are the *Six Fugues on the name of Bach*, Op. 60, all ingenious enough in their jugglings with musical letters (Schumann's wits had been well sharpened in this respect in youth) and fugal procedures to have found a place in the organ repertory.

In the *Six Studies for pedal-piano*, Op. 56, Schumann turned from fugue to canon. Apart from no. 1, with its disciplined, neoclassical semiquavers, more of the composer's real fingerprints show through this particular form, which he bent to his own needs. In the lyricism of nos. 2 and 4, even the characteristic term *innig* reappears. Nos. 3 and 5 incline towards the world of Mendelssohn's *Songs without Words* (Clara's diary records no. 5 as the one Mendelssohn liked best 'as I thought he would, for this is the one most in sympathy with his own temperament'). No. 6 would be at home in the organ-loft, for evensong. A footnote to the edition Clara prepared for Breitkopf points to the possibility of piano-duet performance for all six (and Op. 58 too), with 'secondo' duplicating the bass line in octaves unless, 'guided by the requirements of the upper part', only the lower note is needed.

The *Four Sketches*, Op. 58, are not without points of imitation, notably in their middle sections. But these simple, ternary form pieces are not primarily contrapuntally motivated, and in style resemble quite a few other Schumann miniatures of the later 1830s.

SIEBEN CLAVIERSTÜCKE IN FUGHETTENFORM, OP. 126

Perhaps it was not by chance that Schumann's next, and last, contrapuntal adventures date from 1853, the year in which he wrote the three piano sonatas for his daughters. The *Sieben Clavierstücke in Fughettenform* are not designated as for the young, and admittedly the lively semiquavers of nos. 4 and 6 (both marked *vivace*) are tricky. Yet in general the pieces are sufficiently short and transparent to suggest that having initiated his children into the mysteries of sonata-form he now wanted to do the same with fugue – perhaps in preparation for the *Forty-eight*. Though more neoclassical than Schumannesque, the subjects are of clear-cut musical character; again, too, as in 1845, Schumann is extremely dutiful in sticking to the point – over-dutiful, even. A bit more episodic contrast and a little more adventure in key would not have come amiss. Nevertheless the artist in Schumann is stronger here than the contrapuntal acrobat. The pieces are grateful to play, especially the fifth in A minor marked *Lento assai, con sentimento*, with its sighing countersubject and later textural dissolving into triplets and semiquavers (nearly all thematic). Perhaps it is not over-fanciful, in view of the *con sentimento* marking, to hail the initial triplet phrase as a deliberate evocation of the Clara motto.

The date of an eight-bar *Canon* in A flat on F. H. Himmel's song 'An Alexis' is not known: it abounds in fearlessly chromatic harmony resulting from close imitation.

MUSIC FOR THE YOUNG

Schumann's delight in the child mind went back to the time when he was the young Clara's 'moonstruck maker of charades'. But whereas his *Kinderscenen* of 1838 were an adult's recollections of a child's world, for adults to play, his *Album für die Jugend*, Op. 68, and *Drei Clavier-Sonaten für die Jugend*, Op. 118, were deliberately planned to put this fanciful world within reach of very young players. The four sets of piano duets can also be included in this category, for though not all are specifically designated as youthful, their technical demands are slight.

The 43 pieces of *Album für die Jugend*, of 1848, are the simplest.

> They have especially wound themselves round my heart, [Schumann explained in a letter to his friend, Reinecke, in October 1848, adding] the fact is that I wrote the first pieces for the album for our eldest child [Marie, born 1 September 1841] on her birthday, and then one after another was added. I felt as though I were beginning to compose again at the very beginning. And you will come upon traces of the old humour here and there.

Incidentally at this time he intended to call the collection *Weihnachtsalbum* (Christmas Album); his publisher persuaded him to make the change when printing the work that December.

Though all was finished within sixteen days, Schumann lavished immense care on the task. His sketch-book reveals considerable revisions, retitlings, and also several total rejections. (*Cuckoo in hiding*, *Lagoon in Venice*, *The Catcher* and *Miniature Waltz* have been posthumously published.) The sketch-books also suggest that at one point he considered including several pieces 'in the manner of' this or that composer, as elementary instruction in style, and furthermore to print some of his 'Rules and Maxims for Young Musicians' (eventually transferred from the *Neue Zeitschrift* to the collection of his literary works he produced in 1853) as well.

Since Marie was only approaching seven, the first few pieces are naturally extremely simple. At no time in the forty-three does Schumann stray beyond keys with three flats or four sharps, though sensibly the pieces grow increasingly difficult, both technically and musically. Even the easiest are very subtly contrasted in touch and in mood. *Soldiers' March* (no. 2) is as detached as the thematically not dissimilar *Ein Choral* (A hymn) (no. 4) is smooth; *Poor Orphan-child* (no. 6) is as sad as *Hunter's song* (no. 7) is cheerful. By technical or imaginative means, Schumann was plainly out to develop expressive characterisation as soon as possible in the young. From *The Wild Rider* (no. 8), *Volksliedchen* (no. 9) and *The Merry Peasant returning from work* (no. 10) onwards he gives melody to the left hand as freely as to the right. By no. 13, prefixed with a couplet about 'dear May', he is risking the key of E major, significantly also used for *Spring Song* (no. 15), marked *Innig zu spielen*, where the left pedal is introduced for the first time for intimate asides. Dynamic shading is also a vital feature of *The Horseman* (no. 23), in which the rider finally gallops off into the far distance. Rhythmic incisiveness is equally important in this piece, which incidentally exemplifies Schumann's curious way throughout the set of using triple rhythm only within a 6/8 pulse. The melodic imitation of *Canonic Song* (no. 27) prepares the player for the greater contrapuntal complexity of *Miniature Fugue* (no. 40), with its fugue artfully derived from the prelude. Different musical interpretations of the same sort of extra-musical idea are juxtaposed in *Italian Sailors' Song* and *Sailors' Song* (nos. 36 and 37), with the Italians portrayed in a tarantella, and in the two pieces called *In the Winter* (nos. 38 and 39). And in *Figurierter Choral* (no. 42) Schumann provides a different musical interpretation of a purely musical idea: the piece is an elaborated and reharmonised F major transposition of the chorale-tune 'Freue dich, o meine Seele' first met in G major in no. 4.

Schumann's original idea of including pieces in the styles of other composers can be detected in *Remembrance* (no. 28), subtitled '4 November 1847'. The date is that of Mendelssohn's death, and the piece (headed *gesangvoll*) borrows the manner of a song-without-words. Though not immediately recognisable on grounds of style, the *Northern Song* (no. 41) has a theme (which launches every two-bar phrase) built out of the letters of Gade's name translated into musical notes – this piece is in a sense a development of the fragment Schumann inscribed in Gade's album, in farewell, when the Danish composer left Leipzig in the early 1840s. Three pieces in the collection are headed only with asterisks. The first (no. 21) is, as Kathleen Dale has pointed out,[1] 'a free improvisation on the phrase "O Dank! ihr habt mich süss erquickt" from the terzetto "Euch werde Lohn in bess'ren Welten" from *Fidelio*'. Nos. 26 and 30 could well conceal other similar secret references. The whole collection is pure Schumann, a composer delighting again in a lost world of youthful fairytale, unstrained by the demands of a large canvas. With great understanding of the young, Schumann insisted on an attractive cover design for the issue by Ludwig Richter, famous for his fairytale illustrations.

DREI CLAVIER-SONATEN FÜR DIE JUGEND, OP. 118

The three *Sonatas for the young* were written in 1853 for Schumann's three eldest daughters, no. 1 for Julie, no. 2 for Elise, and no. 3 for Marie; at

---

[1] In Gerald Abraham, *op. cit.*

the time they were aged 8, 10 and 12 respectively. The first, for Julie, is predictably the shortest and simplest, with everything lying comfortably under a little hand. The first movement is in neat ternary (not sonata) form, the second is a theme and variations, the third (again in ternary form) is a 'doll's cradle-song', and the fourth a rondoletto. Though not as potently Schumannesque as the *Album für die Jugend*, the movements remain fresh-sounding because not unduly protracted. In the second and third sonatas for Elise and Marie, Schumann rightly stretches both technical capability and musical understanding. Unfortunately he also sometimes stretches musical ideas not arresting enough to stand up to prolonged investigation: sonata form, never a natural way of thought for him, is used for first and last movements of both works. But the finale of no. 2 has the title 'Children's party' and that of no. 3 'Child's dream' as extra imaginative aids for the young throughout much that is merely repetitious. The latter, a C major 6/8, is interesting for its recall of the opening theme of Julie's Sonata (no. 1), still in G major and 2/4 though mildly developed while in transit to second-subject territory. In accordance with the traditional lively-ending principle, the tempo marking here is fast: the music itself, however, seems to need more leisure to dream.

The most successful movements in these last two sonatas are the middle ones, where the musical essence is not diluted through protraction. The second movement of no. 2, 'Canon', is a sprightly contrapuntal exercise; the third movement, 'Evening Song', is an innocent, Mendelssohnian keyboard song, useful in developing cantabile tone. A deeper, introspective note is touched in the second movement of no. 3; headed *ausdrucksvoll* (expressive), this is the most truly Schumannesque music of the set, and the right foil for the vivacity of the naïve gipsy dance that follows.

MUSIC FOR FOUR HANDS

Immediately after the *Album für die Jugend* Schumann started writing piano duets — for the first time since 1828 and that set of eight posthumously published, Schubert-inspired *Polonaises* subsequently raided for *Papillons*. With a growing family of his own, the duet medium was irresistible; so, too, was the joy of once more writing miniatures sparked off by poetic imagery after the rigours of counterpoint. The *Bilder aus Osten* (Pictures from the East), Op. 66, were avowedly inspired by Rückert's version of the Arabic *Makamen* of

Hariri; Schumann's own copy of the text was marked with six crosses, but unfortunately he chose not to print clues in the form of descriptive titles for these six impromptus, as he subtitled the pieces. The cycle is anchored to deep flats, tonally, and is unmistakably unified in spirit. On grounds of local colour, the pieces are perhaps even less easily identified as oriental than are the *Spanisches Liederspiel* for voices and piano duet, written shortly afterwards, as Spanish. But this Op. 66 is the most sophisticated of the four duet sets; the remaining three are more obviously aimed at the young in heart, though without any obvious condescension as regards *primo* and *secondo*: pleasures and problems are fairly equally shared. Since 1849 was the year of the 'Barricade Marches' (see p. 66), it is interesting to find four of the *Zwölf vierhändige Clavierstücke für kleine und grosse Kinder* (Twelve Duets for children, small and large), Op. 85, taking march form – or rather, titles. *Geburtstags-marsch* (Birthday March) (no. 1) was first performed by Schumann and his daughter, Marie, as a birthday present for Clara on 13 September of that year. All twelve pieces have a beguiling youthful freshness. *Am Springbrunnen* (By the fountain) is about as close to Liszt, in delight in evocative sonority, as Schumann ever came; the breathtakingly poetic final *Abendlied* (Evening Song) tempted Beecham to score and insert it as additional background music in *Manfred* (for Manfred's soliloquy near the end, 'The stars are forth'). The *Ball-Scenen*, Op. 109, of 1851, and *Kinderball*, Op. 130, of 1850–3, are both dance suites. *Ball-Scenen* starts with a *Préambule* and finishes with a *Promenade*; here Schumann was obviously trying to recapture the magic of *Carnaval*, with dancers in national costume (Polish, Viennese, Hungarian, French and Scottish) instead of *Davidsbund* or *commedia dell' arte* disguise. But the simpler, shorter *Kinderball* suite is much more fresh and buoyant.

Schumann's much earlier (1843) attempt at combining two pianos in the *Andante and Variations*, Op. 46, is not within the province of this book, since the original version was scored for two pianos, two cellos and horn, and was obviously intended for a purely domestic celebration, as the quotation from *Frauenliebe und-leben* (between variations 5 and 6) indicates.

WALDSCENEN, OP. 82

On 14 September 1848 Schumann completed the *Album für die Jugend*. On 29 December he started *Waldscenen* (Forest Scenes), finishing the nine pieces in exactly nine days. Though not written for youthful players, they continue in the same transparent vein, without making heavy technical demands. As indicated by the collective title, Schumann's inspiration on this occasion was forest romanticism, of a kind dear to the heart of every nineteenth-century German artist. Strangeness is blended with the beautiful: besides the flowers and inns and jolly hunters, there are also haunted spots ..nere spirits lurk. Schumann's imagination never failed to respond to, in fact was almost dependent upon, this kind of poetic stimulus. But these nine miniatures also benefit from his intervening experiments in purely musical reasoning: the sequence of thought is frequently more self-generating, more continuous, less sharply sectionalised and contrasted, than in many pieces written a decade earlier.

Originally, each piece carried a poetic motto, though these were removed before publication – except for no. 4, *Verrufene Stelle* (The place of evil fame), still prefaced by Hebbel's

Die Blumen, so hoch sie wachsen,
Sind blass hier, wie der Tod;
Nur eine in der Mitte
Steht da im dunkeln Roth.
Die hat es nicht von der Sonne:
Nie traf sie deren Gluth;
Sie hat es von der Erde,
Und die trank Menschenblut.

(The flowers that grow so high are here as pale as death; only in the middle grows one which gets its dark red not from the sun's glow but from the earth which drank human blood.)

This D minor piece is one of the gems of the set, with stealthy dynamics, piquant chromaticism (note the conflicting major and minor chords near the end) and, last but not least, little darting rhythms like cold shudders, all helping to evoke the mood of unease. No. 7, *Vogel als Prophet* (Bird as prophet), is just as atmospheric. 'Hüte dich! sei wach und munter' (Take care! Be on your guard!) was its suppressed motto, and here the ominous note in the exquisite tracery of the bird's song is emphasised by accented chromaticism and again, darting rhythm. The middle section, in the warm tonic major, is like a prayer for deliverance from evil. No. 1, *Eintritt* (Entry), shows the same subtle delicacy of evocation, with horns of elfland bidding the listener follow. The original inscription here was:

Wir gehn auf tannumzäuntem Pfad
Durch schlankes Gras, durch duft'ges Moos
Dem grünen Dickicht in den Schoss.

(We go on the fir-bounded path, by tall grass and fragrant moss, into
the heart of the green thicket.)

Its companion piece at the end, *Abschied* (more 'domestic', perhaps, in
its sentiment), was first headed:

Leise dringt der Schatten weiter,
Abendhauch schon weht durchs Tal,
Ferne Höhn nur grüssen heiter
Noch den letzten Sonnenstrahl.

(The shadow imperceptibly closes round; the breath of evening drifts
through the valley; only distant peaks salute the last rays of the sun.)

Of the remaining pieces, the two hunting numbers carried
inscriptions from Heinrich Laube's *Jagdbrevier* to explain their different
slants on the hunter's life, his expectancy (no. 2) and fulfilment (no. 8).
(Incidentally, Schumann was soon to return to these Laube poems in a
cycle for male chorus and four horns entitled *Jagdlieder*, Op. 137.) The
lonely flowers, friendly landscape and welcoming inn (nos. 3, 5 and 6)
are full of charm, despite their naïvety.

FOUR MARCHES, OP. 76

In May 1849 the quiet routine of life in Dresden (to which Schumann had
moved from Leipzig at the end of 1844) was shattered by revolution.
While 'Kapellmeister Wagner' was playing an active part among the
republicans, 'making speeches from the Town Hall, causing barricades to
be built after a system of his own, and many other things', as Clara's diary
puts it, Schumann fled to the country to avoid compulsory enrolment in
the street guard. But he strongly sympathised with the democrats, and on
returning in June to a Dresden overrun with Prussian soldiers who had
quelled the uprising, his indignation overflowed into the *Four Marches*,
Op. 76 (also a fifth subsequently published as no. 14 of *Bunte Blätter*). Of
the 'politics, literature and people' cited as motivating forces in a letter to
Clara (quoted on pp. 6–7), so far politics had played the least part. But
now his blood was really up: he insisted on very speedy publication, and
wanted *Dresden 1849* prominently displayed in the heading. Though this
last idea was dropped, the pieces were always known amongst Schumann's friends as the 'Barricade Marches'.

'Popular marches, stately in character. Extremely brilliant and original' was how Clara saw them. The key sequence of E flat, G minor, B flat and E flat suggests that Schumann envisaged them as a cycle. Only no. 3 carries the heading *sehr mässig*. The others are marked *mit grösster Energie*, *sehr kräftig* and *mit Kraft und Feuer*. All are in simple ternary form, with middle sections more flowing in style though not in sharp enough contrast to be marked as trio, alternativo or intermezzo, as was often Schumann's wont. The middle section of the last is the most tell-tale: the key switch from E flat to B major (*molto sostenuto*) brings the fullest salute to the *Marseillaise* Schumann had yet permitted himself. Whether consciously or not, the middle section of no. 1 harks back to the Clara motif – if by design, then surely in salute to Clara's courage in going back into Dresden at the height of the fighting, though far advanced in pregnancy, to fetch their younger children who had been left behind. All four middle sections, in fact, bring keener reminders of the real Schumann than the heroic-militant gestures of the main sections, where, despite ingenious variety of rhythmic patterns within common time, Schumann rarely manages to make a frontal attack on the emotions – as Wagner so surely would have done with a memorable tune. But the less flamboyant no. 3, headed 'Lager-Scene' (Camp scene), has its fanciful touches, not least the stealthy ending.

BUNTE BLÄTTER, OP. 99 ALBUMBLÄTTER, OP. 124

The *Bunte Blätter* (Motley leaves) appeared as Op. 99 in 1851. But the fourteen pieces were not written at that time as a set. Instead, Schumann salvaged what he considered the best of a number of short pieces of various dates which, for one reason or another, had not found their way into any of his previous publications. He spoke lightly of this music as 'chaff', but hoped it might be of some interest as a miscellany of 'musical moods'. The collective title refers to his original idea of publishing the pieces separately with coloured covers appropriate to the mood in question. The first three were to have been green.

The earliest is no. 6, a shapely little slow waltz inexplicably rejected from *Carnaval*, which dates it as around 1834. Six of the other pieces grew from 1838–9 and the time when Schumann whiled away many a lonely hour in Vienna at the keyboard. Of these no. 1 has the special interest of having been written as a Christmas greeting for Clara:

You will grasp its significance [he wrote to her]; do you remember Christmas Eve three years ago and how passionately you embraced me? You seemed to be almost frightened at the way in which you let yourself go sometimes. It is different now, for you are assured of your love and know me through and through.

Nos. 2, 4 and 5, in their concentrated expressiveness, continue the style of the 1837 *Fantasiestücke*. Through its key, no less than its title, no. 9 could well have been a rejected *Novellette*, perhaps too transparent for the big Op. 21 group. No. 10 in B flat minor combines the intensity of the Op. 28 *Romanzen* with the neoclassicism of the *Vier Clavierstücke*, Op. 32: it is said to have grown from the remains of two wrecked fugues.

Of the post-1840 pieces, the latest is no. 14, *Geschwindmarsch* (quick-march), a revised version of one originally intended for the rousing set of 'Barricade Marches', Op. 76. Its defiant mood (intensified by biting appoggiaturas) is in sharp contrast to another march, no. 11 in D minor, whose slow, solemn tread reinhabits the world Schumann had explored in the slow movement of his Piano Quintet, Op. 44, of the preceding year. Of the rest, the extended G minor *Scherzo*, no. 13, was salvaged from a projected C minor symphony of 1841, and betrays the fact in less pianistic texture. Since 1841 was Schumann's first great orchestral year, the chromatically inflected *Abendmusik*, no. 12, written in minuet tempo, might also have originated as an orchestral sketch. The simple, plaintive no. 4 of the same year is nevertheless wholly pianistic: the fact that it reverts to the Clara motif, this time under-pinned by alternating F sharps and E sharps (Florestan and Eusebius?), suggests that Brahms may have chosen it for other, more personal, reasons than its perfect shape as the theme of his Op. 9 Variations.

Apparently musicians found the Op. 99 'musical moods' of interest, for Schumann published a second selection of twenty pieces, collectively entitled *Albumblätter*, as his Op. 124 in 1854, the last year of his working life. As the preceding year had found him making an anthology of his most valued critical essays, perhaps he had some premonition of approaching end. For this second salvage operation of keyboard minia-tures he allowed himself to browse still further into the past, resulting in a collection perhaps slighter than Op. 99 but more fanciful. Nos. 1, 3, 12, 13 and 15 go right back to 1832, the year of *Papillons*, for which no. 3, with its prophetic cross-rhythms, was in fact originally intended. No. 17, *Elfe*, was not only rejected from *Papillons* but also from *Carna-val*, whose 1835 date it was given. The other *Carnaval* rejections are no. 4 (a cunning A minor approach to the motto), no. 11 (with a startling *Reconnaissance*-like key-switch in its middle section), and no. 15, whose early date of 1832 comes as a reminder that Schumann was engrossed in variations on Schubert's *Sehnsuchtswalzer* immediately before the impulse metamorphosed into *Carnaval*. Schubert's influence can again be detected in no. 7, entitled *Ländler*, of 1836, and again in no. 10, called *Walzer*, dating from as late as 1838. No. 2 is interesting as the only extract from the 1833 variations on the *allegretto* from Beethoven's Seventh Symphony which Schumann himself chose to publish.[1] This revised version of 1835 is headed *Leides Ahnung* (Premonition of sorrow), the 'Leid' no doubt suggested by the falling phrase which pervades the piece. No. 8, of 1837, is entitled *Leid ohne Ende* (Sorrow without end), and here the Clara motif reappears with much of the same emotional intensity as in the C major *Fantasia* of 1836. It can hardly be coincidental that no. 16, a Mendelssohnian *Schlummerlied* (Slumber song), and no. 6, called *Wiegenliedchen* (Cradle-song) should have appeared in 1841 and 1843, respectively, when Schumann's first two daughters were born. And not surprisingly the concluding no. 20, called *Kanon*, dates from 1845, when Schumann was intoxicated with counterpoint.

FANTASIESTÜCKE, OP. 111

Schumann's move to Düsseldorf in 1850 was an enormous fillip to his imagination: by the end of that year he had produced two major masterpieces, the 'Rhenish' Symphony and Cello Concerto, and some of the same impetus overflowed into 1851, the year of the *Fantasiestücke*, Op. 111. As if to leave no doubt that the three pieces were conceived as a set and meant to be played in sequence he wrote the word *attacca* at the end of nos. 1 and 2. Moreover the key-scheme is even closer than was his wont in cycles. Whether the choice of C minor for an Op. 111 was a deliberate salute to Beethoven or not, it rules the set – even returning in the middle section of no. 2 in A flat major.

At the start Schumann seems to remember his earlier *Fantasiestücke*, Op. 12: the turbulent chromaticism eventually leads to a direct quotation from *In der Nacht*. But this first piece shows a change of style in the fourteen intervening years: the material is more plastic, the flow self-generating so as to reveal new facets of the ideas, rather than symmetrically repetitive. Compared with Op. 12, this no. 1 is a premonition of later Brahms (whom in 1851, at 18, Schumann had not yet met).

1 The complete work was published for the first time in 1976 (Henle Verlag).

No. 2 in A flat is much more redolent of an early love in so far as its idyllic main theme is concerned: both in melodic disposition and texture it is the nearest Schumann ever came to a Schubert impromptu. The *più mosso* middle section returns to the chromatic C minor of the first piece. With its melody woven into arpeggio accompaniment in the middle register of the keyboard, it is more recognisably Schumannesque, though not with imagination working at white heat.

For the third piece Schumann returns to C minor and to a more familiar four-square style. The main theme has a down-to-earth, diatonic robustness that deserves more imaginative textural presentation. The pleading motif running through the gentler contrasting section is enhanced by the upward leap to its accented leading note: despite the modulation, there is more than a suspicion here of that reliance on patterning against which Schumann had constantly to be on guard at all periods of his life.

GESÄNGE DER FRÜHE, OP. 133

Schumann thought highly of what proved to be his last completed piano work, these *Songs of the Morning* written in 1853, the year before his attempted suicide and total mental breakdown. Modern reseach has tracked down the initial source of inspiration to Hölderlin's *Diotima* poems, but Schumann himself certainly allowed no hint of this to reach the public through titles or mottoes. To his publisher he merely described the work as 'five characteristic pieces for pianoforte dedicated to the poetess Bettina [Brentano]. They are pieces depicting the approach and waxing of the morning but more as expression of feeling than painting'. Not only this programme-clue but the key sequence too (D major, B minor, A major, F sharp minor, D major) shows Schumann as wedded as ever to the unified cycle. But on grounds of style these pieces give an idea of the path Schumann might have taken had not illness intervened.

In artistic worth, the set is variable. No. 3, presumably designed to depict morning in its fullest glory, is the most disappointing: here the dotted rhythmic pattern of the first bar persists with obsessive monotony throughout the entire piece. But nos. 2 and 4, where melody and accompaniment are intertwined in a totally different way from Schumann's mid-1830 norm, must have made a very strong impression on the young Brahms, who met Schumann for the first time in the autumn of 1853. The texture is much like that of some of Brahms's later intermezzos. The greater intensity of the three central numbers is contained within a calmer D major prelude and postlude, both marked *tranquillo*. No. 1 has a shapely line and a fine, natural flow made the more interesting by irregular phrase-lengths; even its most chromatically tinged harmonies grow logically and effortlessly from the part-writing. The piece could be a gentle hymn of praise for the birth of a new day. No. 5 has less easily definable spiritual undertones: here the main theme is soon absorbed by, and eventually totally dissolved into, smooth-flowing semiquavers. All five pieces are dominated by their opening motif, but in a more artfully continuous way that avoids exact repetitions just as much as sharp sectional contrasts. The ideas themselves may lack the gleaming freshness of Schumann's early youth. But there is a compensatory, introspective mellowness in this his last completed work.

VARIATIONS ON A THEME IN E FLAT

A letter to Joachim, dated 7 February 1854, ended ominously:

> We have been away a week now without sending you or your companions a sign. But I have often written to you in spirit, and there is an invisible writing, to be revealed later, underlying this letter. . . . I will close now. It is growing dark.

On the night of 10 February, the darkness arrived. A single note drumming in Schumann's head eventually dissolved into music 'more wonderfully beautiful and played by more exquisite instruments than ever sounded on earth', causing him to jump out of bed on the night of 17 February to write down a theme sent him by 'the angels'. Though in fact no more than a subconscious memory of the slow movement of his very recently completed Violin Concerto, it served as starting point for one last essay in variation form. When on 27 February the voices of angels turned to demons he threw himself into the Rhine, but even after his rescue wrote one more variation before entering an asylum in March. Both theme and variations reflect this background, their naïvety eventually giving way to the crude. The simple triplet and semiquaver embroidery of variations 1 and 3 respectively, the canon of var. 2, and the reharmonisation of var. 4, are those of a student; the bizarre discords in the accompaniment of var. 5 speak all too clearly of a mind strained to breaking point. A tragic farewell – yet how apt that Schumann should have made it through his long-cherished variation form, and still more, at his beloved piano. In Elysium, perhaps his greatest comfort of all was that this angelic theme was brought to the glory he envisaged for it in a set of variations for piano duet by his chosen member of the younger generation, Johannes Brahms.

Principal Works Mentioned